The New Era of Network Marketing

---

*How to escape the rat race and
live your dreams in the new economy*

Dave Nelson

Edited by Ben Phillips

ISBN: 1500603007
ISBN 13: 9781500603007

CONTENTS

PART THREE

Mind-set & Miscellaneous
67

CONTENTS

Escaping the Matrix
with Network Marketing

"When a man for whatever reason, has the opportunity to lead an extraordinary life, he has no right to keep it to himself."

—JACQUES-YVES COUSTEAU

I N THE 1999 BOX OFFICE HIT *The Matrix*, we meet Neo, an everyday office worker who discovers the "truth": the truth that modern-day America is in fact a virtual simulation, being used to turn human beings into batteries, orchestrated by a higher intelligence. Some would say that this plot is philosophically symbolic of the lives lived by many in today's world—lives of mundane repetition, like mice on a wheel, sustaining a system that is only conducive to corporations and "higher powers"

On a surface level, most people appreciated the movie as a cutting-edge action sci-fi thriller with incredible fight scenes and revolutionary graphics. But I believe that somewhere deep down, there was something about this tale of self-discovery that resonated with you, whether you consciously realized it or not. You knew there was an underlying philosophical message that spoke directly to you—about the system into which most of us have been born. In the words of Morpheus, "You've felt it your entire life, that there's something wrong with the world. You don't know what it is, but it's there, like a splinter in your mind, driving you mad." I believe that most of us live our daily lives with the nagging sensation of that "'splinter in our mind'" We are frustrated with the life we live and feel that we were put here to do and to achieve more. And if you look at movies like *The Godfather, Scarface, Troy,* and *The Wolf of Wall Street*—hey, just about any movie ever made that we resonate with—you will notice that they all have the same underlying idea of escaping a life of mediocrity and striving for more. In fact I believe that you can find this trend throughout human history. We feel it intuitively, desire it, and are intrigued by it. I believe this fight for freedom is ingrained within our DNA. For many of us it is more than a desire; it's a mission, and if these words ring true for you, then this industry will serve you well.

Whether you call it *The Rat Race* or *The Matrix,* it's a life lived by most, and it is more accurately described as "an existence." Most of us in today's developed world wake to an alarm clock five days a week for fifty weeks of the year and administer ourselves with caffeine to give us the high we need to start the day that we don't want to attend. We sit in traffic; we work; we consume; we watch TV; we go to sleep; we pay our taxes; and we repeat it all over again. As a result of the global financial crisis, which is showing no signs of improvement, this lifestyle is becoming more and more common. People are stressed, sick, and forced to work extended hours *just* to pay their bills and keep their heads above water. That's why I, along with many other business experts across the planet, see network marketing as one of the single most powerful vehicles that can provide a legitimate pathway out of this *matrix* we find ourselves trapped in.

This is how I see it: the so-called "matrix" that has us living a life of frustration and desperation can be divided into five distinct categories, each one related to and negatively affecting the others. All too often I see people struggling in all five of these areas, and very few have a platform to change the pattern and break free.

1 – **Poor physical health**
2 – **Poor financial health**
3 – **Poor mind-set**
4 – **Poor relationships**
5 – **A poor philosophy/spirituality**

1. **Poor Physical Health**

    It's no secret that people are sicker than they have ever been. Never before has mankind had more knowledge and understanding of the human body and what it needs to function, yet we still have the most health problems in recorded history. Just like Mum said: if you don't finish your vegetables you won't get any dessert. Well, now that we're older, we realize that if you don't master your health, you won't get to enjoy the other areas of life. Because of this, I believe that the greatest wealth is health, and it should be one of our highest priorities. When our health is out of balance, it has a domino effect on the rest of our life. Symptoms like tiredness, illness, obesity, and insomnia go on to affect our ability to function well and to create wealth. They go on to affect our mind-set, making us cranky, unable to concentrate, and with little enthusiasm for life. In a state like this it's easy to make bad choices that we wouldn't usually make. Over time the cumulative effect of all this begins to impact negatively on our friendships, our work, and our life in general. Essentially, our health affects *everything*.

2. **Poor Financial Health**

    It's also no secret that people are struggling financially more than ever before, and economists are saying that this is not another depression but, rather, the new economy.

People are feeling the pinch, and one thing is for sure: approaching the new economy with the same tactics that worked in the old economy will end in disaster. It's been shown that financial problems are instrumental to the gradual accumulation of stress in our lives. Stress is like a harmful toxin to the human body, which has numerous negative effects on our overall health. So could it also be said that the greatest health is wealth? When we are in financial pain, we begin to lose sight of who we really are, and we can become desperate. We change our personality as our survival instincts kick in, and we break rules that we once held ourselves to. I don't believe that money is the root of all evil; however, I do believe that a lack of money is the cause of much of the world's pain.

3. **Poor Mind-set**
Modern society is faced with an ever-increasing number of people suffering with depression, anxiety, and a long list of other mental struggles. A poor mind-set can be a by-product of a person's poor financial and physical health. To add to that, people don't read enough these days; instead, they are glued to Facebook or watch reruns of *Gossip Girl,* and play games like *Angry Birds* on their phone to serve as a distraction from their unfulfilling lives.

As a result of this kind of lifestyle, the vast majority of people's thoughts are negative, self-limiting, and often envious of other people. This thinking is fear based and couldn't be further from what is in alignment with prosperity and love. In fact it attracts the complete opposite.

4. Poor Relationships

Whether we like it or not, we share this planet with around seven billion people, and I am certain that we are here to learn to work and live together in harmony. I firmly believe that in some shape or form, we are destined to come together as "one," and that true happiness and fulfilment come from human interaction. If this weren't the case, there are enough planets out there for us all to have been put on our own planets with the freedom to do and act as we please, regardless of the consequences. But that isn't the case, so we must learn to deal with the situation at hand! Much of the frustration of human existence comes from a general lack of understanding and from being void of compassion for our fellow man. And so much of the emotion, pain, and anger that we feel on a daily basis is due to the words and actions of other people. So working out how to connect with other people will alleviate so much of the suffering we experience as individuals and will also have a ripple effect for the entire planet. The trend of people living lives that are cut off from one another is demonstrated by the widespread decline in people skills like communication. Face-to-face conversations have been replaced by social media, and texting is routinely used to communicate when the other person is within hearing range! It doesn't get any better at school either, where instead of being taught how to think, we learn how to read and regurgitate the information that's written in textbooks. At home we are programmed by low-grade TV shows, and instead of a sense of appreciation, we now have a shocking sense of entitlement. Essentially, we've lost our way and are trying to be who we think society says we should be rather than simply who we are, and as a result we wind up building someone else's dream at what we call our *job*. I think it's fair to say that the new depression isn't purely financial; it's reflective of our collective state of mind.

5. **A Poor Philosophy and No Spirituality**
   Now I understand that the movie *The Matrix* is talking about things far deeper than what we experience in our everyday lives, and I don't want to get completely off track. But I will say that I believe we are an advanced species, and there's a lot more "out there" that science is yet to discover, let alone understand. I do believe in oneness, and I believe that most of us have missed this and are instead far too focused on the *I*, or *self*, not on serving others.

You only need to take a look at the statistics to see that the majority of the population is stuck in at least one of these traps. The by-product of living within a system that isn't designed to develop prosperity is frustrated mindless drones in search of an escape. But the rut they have dug themselves into over the years is often too deep to escape, and they're too distracted and unaware to get up and do something about their problems.

But what does the majority of society being broke, sick, and crazy have to do with network marketing and the movie *The Matrix*? Well, although at first glance this business model may look like nothing more than a multi-level recruiting scheme, there is a reason why the most successful people on the planet are endorsing the industry. Not only can it provide you with a vehicle to reach the end goal of financial and time freedom, but along the journey you will have to break free of each matrix mentioned above. You will have to master your mind-set and the money game and get your health on track, and you will certainly have to master the art of dealing with people. Network marketing companies don't just create millionaires;

they create leaders. Their job is far greater than simply selling products; they are self-development companies, passionate about unlocking their representatives' full potential. You will develop more leadership skills and experience more personal growth in network marketing than in any other industry in the world, and most importantly you will learn to deal, connect, and communicate with people. You will learn about the universal laws of prosperity and success, and if you're with a health-based network marketing company, you will become a product of the product. If not, most leadership programs today now make health and nutrition a key area of focus because they understand its power and the butterfly effect it has on every area of life.

Why do we need residual income?

Building a successful network marketing business is like having a residual income-building machine. True financial freedom from the "physical matrix" or "trap" lies in your ability to create residual income, meaning that you are no longer forced to trade your time in exchange for money. There are plenty of income options out there, but only a select few can produce residual cash flow. Residual cash flow means getting paid again and again and again from work you did at one time. After a big year as a top real estate agent, you begin the next year back at square one and have to start all over again. Residual income is a far more lucrative option, and when you add to that the travel advantages, the tax savings, and the ability to work from home, there really is no other industry quite like it, and the masses are beginning to realize this.

I believe that network marketing is liberating people from a twenty-first-century prison of poor health, slavery to the dollar, a poor mind-set, and little understanding of others and the world. If you're new to this industry, be prepared to change every area of your life for the better—not just your bank statement. You will leave some people behind, and others could even resent you for your success and personal growth because it highlights their failures and missed opportunities. But pay no attention to them; if you want to fly, sometimes you have to let go of the weight holding you back.

Now I understand that this chapter may seem a little dark and gloomy; it isn't meant to be. It's a very exciting time to be alive. People are beginning to wake up, make changes, and evolve. Despite popular belief, because we are in the information age I believe the world is getting better. I believe that the future is extremely bright for leaders, entrepreneurs, and especially network marketers!

My Story

"You can't connect the dots looking forward; you can only connect them looking backwards. So you have to trust that the dots will somehow connect in your future."

—STEVE JOBS

AS YOU HAVE PROBABLY GATHERED FROM THE INTRODUCTION, there is nobody more passionate about this industry than I. I was another multilevel marketing (MLM) rags-to-riches story. At twenty-three, I had been fired from my thirteenth different job; I had accrued $20,000 in debt; I had a horrible attitude toward life in which I believed that the world was out to get me; and I wanted no part in it. I remember being so broke that I would fill up my car with twenty dollars at a time and never let the revs go above 2000 rpm. Needless to say, the air conditioner was strictly never used as it chewed up too much gas, costing me more money that I didn't have! I would never answer a private number because I knew it was someone chasing me for money, and at twenty-three I was still searching the back of the couch and going through my parents' dresser drawers looking for loose change. It was the lowest point in my life, and I was miserable. I hated the person I was; I was embarrassed by who I had become; and it goes without saying that the future looked bleak.

It all began after barely scraping through high school. I wanted to make good money and become successful, so I decided to take up a trade as a landscape builder, following the recommendation from my parents and teachers, who called it "the lucrative option." Well, if lucrative means being worked like a slave to dig holes for endless hours in ungodly summer temperatures and carry an endless supply of really heavy things, only to wind up without enough money to buy basic necessities at the end of each week, then I guess they were spot on! There was no way I could live like this. I tried job after job, looking for inspiration and a vehicle that would provide me with a good life and happiness, but it was nowhere to be found. I knew that if I wanted to live well and to be a success, I had to work for myself, but this was what created the debt in the first place. Having been involved in multiple ventures that never took off, I was your typical story of working all week to get blind drunk on the weekend. I hated every minute of what I was going through and asked myself, "Is this really all there is to life?" Little did I know that the pain I was experiencing was my greatest gift as it would spark a deep fear of mediocrity that would grow into a relentless work ethic and the ability to take risks and make drastic changes.

So not knowing what to do next, I jumped on a cruise ship to escape the "matrix" I found myself trapped in. But among all of the promised opportunity and chance to "'live the dream'" of working abroad, the commercials and sales pitches failed to provide details of what working on a cruise ship was actually like. I soon discovered the slave-labor pay rate and the poor living and working conditions, and after three months, I found myself in an even bigger rut than when I started. But fortunately my time was up; I had somehow paid my dues or cleared my karmic debt, and I was introduced to network marketing. I had heard about the business model before and wasn't skeptical at all. At first I thought it was just a small-time side venture and didn't take it too seriously, but that changed very quickly when I did some further reading and saw some of the industry figures for myself. I had no idea that some of the Tupperware salespeople were profiting $200,000 plus per year, and there were multimillionaires left, right, and center. But once I did, I very quickly changed my commitment levels! To make a long story short: I had found my golden ticket, and for the first time in my life I had committed 100 percent of my efforts into something. All of my dreams and aspirations were alive again. I had hope, and I was excited.

Starting out, I thought to myself: *If they can do it, then why can't I?* And I give you this question to consider: *Why not you?* This mentality got me through the tough times, and instead of throwing in the towel or blaming my up-line, the industry, the economy, or my family, I just kept saying to myself, "If they figured this out, then so can I." I felt like I was playing a big video game in which I had to get better in order to move to the next level. I had climbed the wrong tree many times and had worked hard in a job or industry that had no fruit at the top. But in this game I knew that if I reached the top sector, I would have everything I had ever imagined, and I could live my dream life.

Getting started was extremely tough—I wasn't fired from thirteen consecutive jobs by accident. I had a bad attitude and lots of limiting beliefs that didn't serve me. In my first three months, I didn't sign a single person that wasn't family. This destroyed my ego, and my frustration levels were through the roof, but I was well aware that I had no other options. Working a job in today's economy was never going to give me the freedom of life that I desired, and I had no money or skills to launch my own regular business, so I stuck it out. It was at the three-month mark that I had my life-defining moment. I felt like I had an "instant awakening" while reading *Secrets of the Millionaire Mind* by T. Harv Eker. The entire book busted my ego and slapped me around, but there was one point in particular that really spoke to me: *Your inner world creates your outer world, and everything you have today is a result of what happened in your mind.* This was the moment when I realized that I, and only I, had created the mess I was in: not my family, not the economy, not my education, not anything, or anyone—just me! I had to face myself and my demons, which was a difficult thing to do, but at the same time, it was exciting. For the first time in my life, I felt like I had control, and I was the architect of my future, no longer dictated to by the circumstances around me. I finally took responsibility for my life and made the necessary changes to my mind-set to change the outcomes.

So with this new understanding of the power of my own mind and a new lease on life, I began reading and developing myself intensely. It became like an addiction to me, and by the time I turned twenty-six (just two and a half years later), I found myself living a dream life. My best buddies from school that I got started at the beginning were all doing the business full time and making six-figure incomes. I purchased a Ferrari and bought expensive watches and designer suits and now stayed at high-end resorts with butlers and chefs. I also made investments into multiple ventures and was living in a beachside condo on the beautiful Gold Coast. People now respected me and saw me as an inspiration. I was no longer the town drunk or the idiot that managed to be popular by being funny and doing stupid things. Now I was on stage in front of several thousand people, sharing my story. My life had truly turned itself upside down in the space of two years.

Now I am not as materialistic as I may sound. The true beauty of creating wealth isn't the money or the material things it buys but, rather, the stress it removes from your life. Not only has money eliminated most of my problems, but the mind-set that I had to develop in order to make the money now puts me at peace. I sometimes look back to where I was three years ago: out of control, breaking down in tantrums, and smashing everything in sight— compared to where I am now: living the life of my dreams, in peace and with nothing but love for the world. Once you reach a certain level of success and you are no longer coming from a place of struggle and desperation, I believe you start to become comfortable with who you truly are. Today, although I am very focused and highly driven to succeed, I can switch off and have a good laugh. I don't take anything too seriously, and I am usually clowning around. I'm blessed to be pretty carefree outside of work and to be able to enjoy all areas of my life right now.

No matter what I achieve or what heights I reach, network marketing will always be something that I love and stay involved in. It saved and changed my life; therefore, I know what it can do for others, and for that reason, I will be forever an advocate and supporter of the industry.

But enough about me—you can follow me at davenelson.tv for that.

Let's get on to the topic of this book!

A successful entrepreneur and good friend of mine taught me the elite performance triangle that is made up of three points: skills, system, and mind-set. The idea is that for any organization to reach an elite level, it requires all three sections to be mastered. I believe this to be relevant to our industry, so I have dedicated parts two and three of the book to covering these three areas.

I wrote this book to add value to:

- ➤ new reps that are just getting started and looking for direction and support;

- ➤ people who may be interested in the industry and need more information; and

- ➤ experienced reps looking to leverage off my experience, skills, and ideas.

Writing this book was exciting. I am passionate about the industry, and I'm driven to play a key role in its expansion and ever-growing public awareness. But like taking on any new challenge, I had the same fears, doubts, and hesitations that anyone would have. I mean, I'm certainly not the top earner in the industry; in fact, I'm relatively new, having only been involved for three years. Some would say that I am too young and inexperienced in life at twenty-six, but on the other hand, I feel that I have been able to achieve a high level of success in a faster time frame and at a younger age than most. Thanks to the "'Amazon revolution," I've been able to take a journalistic perspective of the industry by reading a wide range of books and studying what the top companies and organizations have done over the last thirty years, making now the perfect time for me to put together the pieces of the puzzle and write this book.

My childhood hero was Arnold Schwarzenegger, and I am still blown away by what he has achieved in one lifetime. One of the things I noticed was that during his career he wasn't ready to become one of the biggest actors of his time. His acting was awful, and his accent made him difficult to understand, but he took action anyway and became a virtual overnight success and the highest paid actor in the world during his prime. He wasn't ready to be the governor of California either, but he took action anyway and had a relatively successful career serving two terms. So when I hesitated in writing this book, I took inspiration from my hero and wrote it anyway. Now I only hope that this book is the next *Terminator* or *Twins* and not a book that goes down the toilet in the same way as Arnold's disaster movies, like *Jingle All the Way*. I also hope this example inspires you to take action, *even if you're not ready!*

Your partner in prosperity,

Dave Nelson

The Old Era of Network Marketing

"In history, a great volume is unrolled for our instruction, drawing the materials of future wisdom from the past errors and infirmities of mankind."

—EDMUND BURKE

BEFORE BEGINNING THIS CHAPTER, I WANT to make something clear. The people involved in what I refer to as the Old Era of network marketing did a fantastic job. They built this platform to more than $100 billion per year and paved the way for people like me to be granted with this incredible opportunity. The Old Era established network marketing's strong reputation that we enjoy today and cemented its position as a respected business model. The entrepreneurs who pioneered this industry created financial and lifestyle freedom for tens of thousands of people across the globe and put network marketing on the map as a legitimate, ethical, and great way to create wealth.

But just like any multibillion-dollar industry, network marketing has had its share of flaws and bad practices that have attracted negativity and stigma. It is now the responsibility of you and me (the New Era) to unite together and change the face of this industry for the future. Instead of belittling other MLM companies and their representatives, we should embrace them because we all fight for the same end cause and are all

1

crusaders of the New Era of network marketing. And mark my words: in coming years, it will be beautiful to watch as we head into what Randy Gage has dubbed, "the golden era of network marketing."

Here are some of the techniques and common practices of independent representatives that were used during the Old Era of network marketing and that created much of the stigma. (And while some of these things still happen today, we have the opportunity to change the image of the industry for the future.) The following is a list of what *not* to do:

- We saw plenty of untactful desperation and low-quality network marketers verge on begging for people to sign up. They pleaded with desperation and preached with passion, harassing everyone they came into contact with, including their social media contacts. Obviously this type of action didn't serve their business or the industry.
- The desperation and neediness led to false promises and lies that ranged from, "I'll build it for you," to "You won't have to do anything." They sold stories of people doing nothing and getting rich, made false income claims, and said that the product would practically sell itself. (If that were the case, the entire marketing industry would be obsolete.)
- We saw Oscar-Award-worthy acting that had everyday people attempting to play the role of a big businessman, virtually overnight.
- We saw deception and false pretense among friends. Everyone has heard the classic story of the invitation to dinner that was followed by an unexpected appearance of the white board with an accompanying pitch. Don't do it! We have nothing to hide—so be proud and have integrity.
- We saw new reps make the mistake of thinking that the day they became network marketers was also the day they became business

experts, life coaches and philosophers, and all of a sudden they could tell everyone how they should live.

- We saw people alienate friends and family and anyone who didn't join their organization.
- We saw the cheesy spam e-mails consisting of generic scripts that were sent out to databases asking, "How would you like to make $500,000 in your first year?" (When the rep that sent the e-mail made an annual check of $4,000.) It doesn't work. Instead, it damages your name, the company's reputation, and the industry.

What the companies did wrong:

- Companies front-loaded, making people buy up to tens of thousands of dollars' worth of product that they would probably never sell.
- There were high monthly fees and large minimum monthly maintenance orders to stay active in the business.
- They offered lucrative cash deals to bring in people from other organizations.
- Many were not set up properly and didn't have a product, which saw them walk a fine line between a legitimate business and a pyramid scam.

These are some of the things that I believe we, as a group and as representatives of the New Era of network marketing, can work on weeding out of the industry. So get your MLM pest-control suits on; we are going to clean up the image of network marketing one rep at a time! The Direct Sales Association (DSA) and organizations like the Federal Trade Commission (FTC) are already hard at work, implementing new regulations to ensure that companies are maintaining a high standard of business ethics. Fortunately, 99 percent of the things people hated about network marketing no longer occur, so it's an exciting time to be involved in the industry moving forward.

The Old Era economy:

What is incredible about the Old Era of network marketing is its growth. At a time when the economy was relatively healthy, the direct sales industry grew to heights of $100 billion. The great American dream was alive and well throughout most of the Western world, meaning that you could get an average job, buy a home, and retire by age fifty-five—with a pension and benefits. Property markets were booming, the economy was strong, and there was plenty of opportunity in retail, franchising, and small business. In spite of these factors, the network marketing industry continued to thrive. My question to you is this: *If people were flocking to network marketing during economically stable times, when an extra income was likely not needed, then what type of growth do you expect in times of* economic disaster? Let me tell you—we're set for the network marketing Golden Age. Economics forecaster Paul Zane Pilzer believes that the real growth of the industry has barely begun and says that it's showing no signs of ever slowing down. Not many methods of wealth creation are working these days; in fact, other business models are falling apart. I believe that some people will join network marketing in a game of last man standing, and that a certain number of people will be forced to utilize a direct sales model when they reach a point of frustration and desperation with the current insufficient system that they are following.

But despite its progress, there's still considerable work to be done in order to awaken the masses to the opportunity that network marketing holds.

The industry's public opinion throughout the Old Era was predominantly that network marketing was a pyramid scheme. These people obviously weren't reading *Forbes, Fortune,* or any kind of business book or magazine for that matter, and they quite possibly still thought that the world was flat. The idea that a $167 billion industry could be an illegal scheme is absolutely ludicrous. But while on the topic, let's quickly cover what a pyramid scheme *actually* is. It usually refers to a business model that has no product. The commissions that people make are based on people signing up rather than on the sale of a product. For those not familiar with network marketing, here's a simple example using a business model that everyone on the planet is familiar with: a McDonald's franchise. Just imagine that the stores existed, but they had no customers. So no one bought their fries, burgers, or drinks; the stores were always empty. Yet the owners of the McDonald's franchise continued to make money and survived by selling more franchises, which in turn continued to sell more franchises—and so on. All the while, no product was ever sold. This would be a pyramid scheme. Legitimate network marketing companies, on the other hand, often sell a higher quality product than can be found on the shelves of a retail store. This is because the network marketing business model is more efficient and cuts out the person in the middle, providing more time and money to spend on product development. This is not possible in the retail model, which must account for extra costs for marketing, shop staff, shop overhead, and many other things. In network marketing you eliminate all of these costs by buying directly from the company. The opportunity to refer business is not what makes this business a pyramid scheme; it's what makes it the fairest and most equal business opportunity on the planet. When you buy a McDonald's franchise, you only have the ability to sell a product. The owners of the McDonald's brand, however, have the ability to sell franchises and products, which essentially means that they are the ones at the top of the tree with all of the opportunity and making all of the money. In network marketing, each rep gets the same opportunity as the owner of the company to not only sell a product but to also sell opportunity, create leverage, and expand and earn like a CEO. This new understanding is making the industry one of the fastest growing in the world, and the network marketing model will soon be accepted in society like a corporate job or franchising (which was also heavily ridiculed when it first began).

The New Era of Network Marketing

"Change is the law of life. And those who look only to the past or present are certain to miss the future." —John F. Kennedy

The New Era of network marketing has evolved over the last sixty odd years and continues to improve in every area. Not only are direct sales representatives becoming more tactful and doing business in a more tasteful way, the companies and products are also improving. The systems are able to grow faster than ever before with the power of the Internet, and the global financial crisis is creating a gold rush for the industry.

Experts believe that what people are calling "the new depression" is in fact the New Era economy, and it is here to stay. Depending on which country you are from will determine whether you are looked after in retirement. In countries like the United States and Australia, if you are from Generation Y and onward, there will be no government-provided pension, and you will need to support yourself.[1] Retirement funds are looking flaky, and economists and financial experts believe that people will be forced to work late into their eighties (or until death).[2] Many large corporations that were once seen as pillars of financial security are now

---

[1] The new depression
http://economyincrisis.org/the-new-depression
http://useconomy.about.com/b/2013/09/18/worst-global-financial-crisis-since-the-great-depression-no-not-really.htm

[2] Retirement prospects
http://www.cbsnews.com/news/breaking-down-gen-ys-2-million-retirement-price-tag/
http://thenewdaily.com.au/money/2014/02/13/retirement-65-youre-dreamin/

downsizing or folding.[3] No longer is just buying property and seeing it double in value quickly a viable plan; it simply isn't happening anymore. In fact I see people often losing value short term. Wall Street and stocks are fickle, and people working "high-end" jobs are seeing their incomes slashed by half.[4] In the New Era, university degrees are becoming outdated, and students will require retraining. New graduates are already experiencing the difficulties of finding a job in their areas of expertise and are often left to find minimum-wage employment after years of study and the accumulation of tens of thousands of dollars' worth of debt.[5]

A modern trend has seen companies outsource work to third world countries, where people are willing to do twice the amount of work for a tenth of the pay. And not far down the track, that cheap labor will be replaced by machines (it's been predicted that 50 percent of jobs will be replaced by

---

[3] Corporations downsizing
http://www.businessinsider.com.au/15-companies-that-tanked-2011-3?op=1#the-owner-of-the-w-boston-hotel-was-bankrupt-six-months-after-opening-the-luxury-hotel-1
http://www.entrepreneur.com/article/201280
http://topyaps.com/top-10-famous-companies-that-went-bankrupt
http://www.forbes.com/sites/sherylnancenash/2012/05/17/is-higher-education-a-giant-pyramid-scheme/

[4] Wages dropping
http://www.cnbc.com/id/29275784
http://www.ft.com/cms/s/0/64f6df6e-0291-11e4-8c28-00144feab7de.html#axzz376T0mQef
http://www.bbc.com/news/business-25977678

[5] University degrees
http://www.hangthebankers.com/why-university-is-a-scam-the-college-bubble/
http://www.forbes.com/sites/jamesmarshallcrotty/2012/03/01/most-college-grads-cant-find-work-in-their-field-is-a-management-degree-the-answer/
http://www.forbes.com/sites/nextavenue/2014/07/07/how-to-stop-stressing-over-your-childs-job-search/
http://www.firstsun.com/tag/the-one-best-thing-college-students-can-do-to-land-a-job-as-of-april-2014-only-16-6-of-college-seniors-had-gotten-a-single-full-time-job-offer/

machines or outsourced over the next ten years).[6] Working for a corporation used to be the safest option, but today it may be the riskiest move you make. The longer you stay loyal to a company, the greater the target on your back becomes each year because you're now entitled to benefits they don't want to pay you, and you expect a pay raise that they don't want to give you. From their perspective it makes no sense to give you a pay raise when they can just as easily hire an intern to do the same work at half of the cost. All of these factors are driving people's wages down as inflation continues to go through the roof. It's workplace and economic factors like these that have led experts like Robert Kiyosaki and many others to believe that in the not-so-distant future, the middle class will have been completely wiped out, and we will live in a world of rich and poor—the vast majority being poor!

Kids these days don't grow up wanting to be network marketers. They want to be an astronauts, business owners, sports stars, or fire fighters. But I believe that things are going to change, and not only will the masses accept network marketing as a legitimate career, it will be seen as one of the most highly paid and sought after professions in the world. I see the highly driven and ambitious students leaving school not to trade stocks or do real estate but to join forces with a network marketing company to obtain wealth. With the extravagant lifestyles and high-caliber leaders this industry is producing, I believe it will be not only accepted but highly respected. People born into Gen Y and later are considered to be the generation of the entrepreneur. They have witnessed the lives their parents lived as a consequence of fitting into the system and working a job, and they don't want to repeat it. They are rebellious, impatient, creative, and tech-savvy, and they hate authority. All these factors lean toward network

---

[6] 50 percent of jobs will be taken over by robots
http://www.abc.net.au/7.30/content/2014/s4014292.htm
http://bgr.com/2014/03/14/bill-gates-interview-robots/

marketing being a perfect fit for millions of the up-and-coming generation. Ironically, these traits are seen as weaknesses in the work force, but they are the greatest strengths in the entrepreneurial world.

The dream of going to school, developing an expertise, working for a big company as an employee, and then retiring is now nothing more than a fantasy. It's a fairy tale that belongs in the kids' section next to *Humpty Dumpty* and *The Three Little Pigs* (they are probably more believable). It's fair to say that change has arrived and is here to stay. While becoming an employee is not a viable option if you are looking to obtain wealth, owning or starting a business in the New Era economy has now become harder than ever before. For example, many of my friends attempted to open their own gyms or clothing companies, but they couldn't compete with the low pricing of the giant chains that already have profitability figured out, including how to create large accounts where they get production and practices done at a much lower rate. The growth of franchising has slowed for the first time in its history: its profits are getting tighter, and often for the owner it now resembles a high-stress job because instead of enjoying the residual income, they are required to work at it.[7] Paying someone else to be the manager now wipes out too much of their already slim profit margins. Small businesses are being wiped out at an increasing rate by large corporations.[8] Additionally, the days of successfully marketing your product or service via infomercials, magazine advertisements,

---

[7] Franchising establishments down
http://www.franchise.org//IFA_NEWS/
    Franchise_Growth_Lags_As_Fiscal_Cliff_Threatens_Expansion/
http://www.smh.com.au/small-business/franchising/sharp-slowdown-threatens-
    franchising-growth-20100803-113vf.html

[8] Globalization
http://www.businessdictionary.com/article/583/
    impact-of-globalization-on-small-businesses/

and television commercials are nearly over.[9] While these methods of marketing are becoming rapidly outdated, person-to-person marketing and selling is thriving. The traditional distribution method that has been relied on throughout the Old Era economy is no longer proving economically viable.[10] Make no mistake, we are in a depression: people are working more and getting paid less. The price of everything is going up, except for people's wages. We are beginning to see a massive divide between wealthy and broke throughout the world, as Robert Kiyosaki points out in his best seller *Rich Dad Poor Dad*. What Kiyosaki refers to as the right side of the quadrant (business owners and investors) is becoming increasingly relevant. These are the people who make up just 5 percent of the population yet share in 95 percent of the world's money. This leaves behind 95 percent of the population (the hard-working employees and self-employed) to share in a measly 5 percent of the wealth. It's an undeniable fact that the business landscape has changed, and it's now up to individuals to decide whether they want to cling to the Old Era or make the transition into the New Era as smooth as possible.

It's a historical fact that the greatest entrepreneurial opportunities have always come about during times of adversity and economic depression. For those that lift their heads out of the sand and prepare for the coming

---

[9] Word of mouth advertising
http://www.marketingcharts.com/wp/traditional/2-in-3-marketers-say-word-of-mouth-marketing-more-effective-than-traditional-marketing-38330/
http://www.businessweek.com/debateroom/archives/2011/12/word_of_mouth_is_the_best_ad.html
http://blog.getambassador.com/6-amazing-stats-that-prove-word-of-mouth-marketing-is-here-to-stay/

[10] Retail is dying
http://www.businessinsider.com.au/shopping-malls-are-going-extinct-2014-1
http://www.benzinga.com/personal-finance/financial-advisors/12/04/2516027/trend-watch-traditional-retail-is-dying
http://www.forbes.com/sites/alanhall/2012/12/30/the-internet-is-killing-my-business/

decades, the future can be bright. I believe that this is the case for those who are already in the network marketing profession today. During the Old Era, network marketing opportunities were seen as risky, and jobs were seen as safe, but the tables have turned. In the New Era economy this idea has been flipped upside down. Jobs are now the risky option, and the low-overhead, low-risk opportunity of network marketing is making it the safe option for the future. The beautiful thing about network marketing is that it gets you on to the big business side of Kiyosaki's cash flow quadrant. It allows you to run your own business by selling an existing product and creating leverage from an unlimited number of reps that you can bring into your organization. It provides you with all the benefits of owning a big business and the opportunity to expand to an unlimited level. Unlike starting most businesses, you don't need to outlay considerable money to build systems, develop products, or undertake a marketing campaign. With network marketing, you have a business already set up and ready to go without the overhead and huge start-up costs of a franchise. You also have the ability to expand by referring and bringing on other business owners (known as reps), which is a benefit that you don't get in a franchise model. The network marketing business model has all the benefits of owning a regular business or franchise, without any of the negative aspects. There is no other business model in the world quite like it. I believe it's the purest form of enterprise, and that it is going to save millions of people from financial ruin over the next ten years.

What you are about to read in the following chapter is a list of endorsements by some of the wealthiest people on the planet. Economic forecasters, business authors, and advisors are all talking about the coming growth of this industry. So what does this mean for you, and what does this mean for network marketing distributors? It means exponential growth in income. Currently, the top earners in the industry make over $10 million per year—yes, per year! With the anticipated growth, expect to see network marketing experts earning up to double this! You can expect to see the network marketing giants go from $10 billion in annual sales up to $20 billion or even $30 billion in the next decade, putting network marketing companies up there with Apple, Nike, and other mainstream brands. The industry is changing and fast becoming one of the most respected business models in the world. It's an exciting time to be alive, and it's an even more exciting time to be a part of network marketing. So get excited. It's time to put your head down and your bum up and prepare for the extraordinary growth ahead of us.

Welcome to the golden era!

What the Experts Say

"Being ignorant is not so much a shame, as being unwilling to learn."
—*Benjamin Franklin*

Okay, so just to be clear, I am not an expert on finance, the economy, or business. Instead of taking the necessary time to become an expert in multiple fields, I have instead endeavored to find trends in what the experts are all saying about the future economy and network marketing. What you're about to read is quite extraordinary. It is rare to see such a long list of some of the most successful people from a wide range of industries believe in and endorse the same thing. So before reading their quotations on network marketing and its future, I have a quotation by the great Jim Rohn that I want you to think about:

"When you buy into someone's philosophy, you buy into their life."

So you have to ask yourself the question: *Should I be listening to my broke, deadbeat friends and family when it comes to acquiring wealth and living my dreams? Or should I be listening to people who have actually achieved what I want?* When we start listening to broke people who aren't educated in business or wealth creation, we are at risk of obtaining their lives. So don't be rude, but when you get advice from someone who doesn't have what you want, just smile, thank that person for his or her input, slip on your running shoes, sip your Gatorade, pump the iPod, and run as *fast* as you can in the opposite direction!

Before going any further I must apologize in advance to most of the parents out there today because I know that I am generalizing here, and not all parents are doing this. I know that anyone with children does the very best he or she can with nothing but good intentions, but many parents unknowingly do their children a disfavor by providing financial advice when their knowledge of the Old Era economy no longer applies today. Parents, please let financial experts educate your kids. If your child wanted to be a great pianist, then as a parent you would send him or her for lessons with the best teacher available. So why does this not apply to an area of education that will play one of the most important roles in the rest of his or her life? This may seem a little harsh, but it's the truth. I see far too many kids these days take the wrong advice from their parents and, as a result, wind up miserable in a dead-end career. That might have been a good option twenty years ago, but it can be an awful one today. The game has changed, and if you don't change with it, you will be left behind. Can you imagine someone trying to be a professional tennis player today while still using a tiny wooden racquet? It's essentially the same thing, and while I'm at it, don't take advice on creating financial freedom and residual income from your banker, your doctor, your school teachers, or your financial advisor either. They are fantastic at what they do, but remember that they all make an average living at best and have no skills in creating financial freedom at a young age. In fact don't take advice from anyone other than those who have already achieved exactly what it is that you want. Don't get caught in dogmas or society's opinions, because the masses are broke and miserable. But let me get off the soapbox, and let's take a look at what the experts are saying.

Paul Zane Pilzer - nine-time best-selling author and economic forecaster - when talking about the network marketing industry turning over more than $100 billion per year:
"As impressive as that is, it's not hard to see the real growth has barely begun."

Donald Trump - billionaire businessman and TV celebrity:
"Direct sales is actually one of the oldest, most respected business models in the world and has stood the test of time."

Robert Kiyosaki - best-selling wealth author of all time:
"Network marketing is the business of the 21st century. It gives people the opportunity, with very low risk and low financial commitment to build their own income—generating assets and acquiring great wealth."

Warren Buffett - world's richest man in 2008, investor, and author:
"It was the best investment I ever made."

Darren Hardy - owner and publisher of *Success Magazine:*
"The future of employment is self-employment. Direct selling is one of the few business opportunities that offers average people, with above average ambitions to achieve an above average lifestyle, peace of mind and financial security."

Jim Rohn - world-renowned philosopher and author:
"Network marketing is the big wave of the future; it's taking the place of franchising which now requires too much capital for the average person."

Les Brown - motivational speaker:
"Network marketing has probably produced more millionaires than any other industry in the history of the world."

Brian Tracy - best-selling author:
"The future of network marketing is unlimited, there is no end in sight, it will continue to grow, because better people are getting into it, it will become one of the most respected business methods in the world."

Bill Clinton - former US president:
"You strengthen our country and our economy by not only striving for your own success, but offering opportunity to others."

Tony Blair - former British prime minister:
"Network marketing is a tremendous contribution to the overall prosperity of the economy."

Harv Eker - best-selling author of *Secrets of the Millionaire Mind*:
"If it resonates with you, network marketing can be a dynamite vehicle for wealth. It will only work if you do. But if you do, incomes in range of 20k-50k per month are not uncommon, you will never get rich working on a straight salary for someone else."

Stephen Covey - best-selling author of *The 7 Habits of Highly Effective People*:
"Network marketing has come of age, it is undeniable that it has become a way to entrepreneurship and independence for millions of people."

Randy Gage - entrepreneur, best-selling author of *Risky is the New Safe*
"Now, we are about to enter a golden era of network marketing, in the next few years alone tens of millions of distributors will join the profession."

David Bach - *New York Times* best seller and entrepreneur:
"You don't need to create a business plan or create a product. You only need to find a reputable company, one that you trust, that offers a product or service you believe in and are passionate about."

"When I read in *Fortune* Magazine that Warren Buffett was investing in network marking, I decided I was missing something."

Tom Peters - legendary management expert and author:
"The first truly revolutionary shift in marketing since the advent of 'modern' marketing at P&G and the Harvard business school 50–75 years ago."

Zig Ziglar - world-famous best-selling author and speaker:
"A home based business offers enormous benefits, including elimination of travel, time savings, expense reduction, freedom of schedule, and the opportunity to make your family your priority as you set your goals."

Jim Collins - all-time best-selling business author
"This network marketing business offers the most systematic way for ordinary individuals to achieve economic success."

Seth Godin - best-selling author specializing in marketing
"What works is delivering personal, relevant messages to people who care about something remarkable. Direct Sellers are in the best position to do this."

Ray Chambers - entrepreneur, philanthropist, humanitarian, and owner of Princess House:
"The direct selling business model is one that can level the playing field and close the gap between the haves and have nots."

Randy Gage - stated in his latest book *Risky is the New Safe:*
"It is conceivable that 40 to 50 million new people will become network marketing distributors in the period from 2013 to 2017."

Fortune magazine - "The best kept secret in business."

So after all of this, my message to those who still say that network marketing is a scam is: *get over it!* Don't let a few people's failures in this industry sway your judgement. The people who failed at network marketing probably also failed at just about everything they ever tried. Love it or hate it, the industry has a trajectory set for the top and will play a big role in ensuring the future of the economy and the distribution of goods and services globally.

Finding the Right Company

"It is better to be alone than in bad company." —*George Washington*

Thousands of network marketing companies are launched every decade, but only a few survive to really make it big. So it's therefore very important to choose the right one. Do we opt for a ground-floor start-up company that claims to have the best opportunity for growth? Or do we go for the safe option and join an established network marketing giant?

Well I don't believe there's a one-size-fits-all answer. I have seen people join thirty-year-old companies and make a fortune in their opening year. So don't buy into the myth that you need to be on the ground floor to make money. Also remember that less than 5 percent of network marketing companies survive their first five years of business. If the business goes under, you are left with no residual income—just some great skills.

When it comes to how new or old the ideal company should be, I am going to be neutral and sit on the fence. The truth is that it really doesn't matter. No network marketing company will ever reach saturation in our lifetime! If you are after more security, try to find a DSA-approved company. There are around 250 of them, and you can rest assured, knowing that these companies are compliant and doing the best they can to abide by the laws governing the industry.

Do the products matter? I hear a lot of network marketing experts say that the product doesn't matter, but I don't believe that is entirely true. First of all, if you're just selling an opportunity and don't have a customer base, you run the risk of being deemed a pyramid scheme. So for long-term safety and growth, I recommend finding a company that sells a product that people buy anyway. Just look at Tupperware, makeup, supplements, and grocery companies. They all sell a product that people are already purchasing, which makes the transfer from a retail store to an independent representative a lot smoother. In saying that, if you have an "outside-the-box" product, it can still be effective, but it must have outstanding results with a simple and duplicable explanation for how it works.

Of course when inspecting network marketing companies you need to ensure that they have a reliable distribution system and an effective customer care team. This will save you plenty of time and lots of hassles down the track. It is always best to join a company that fits well with your personality, so attend some meetings, see what the people are like, check out the training, and get a feel for whether it's going to be an appropriate fit for you.

Six things to look for in a network marketing company

1 - Product

There is a huge advantage in getting behind a company with a product that you are passionate about. That's simple. Be sure to look a little deeper and consider things like the following: Is the product perishable? Will people buy the product? Is it reasonably priced in the market? Is it easy to explain? (If the way it works is too scientific and complicated, duplication will be more difficult.) Is it unique? Are people used to buying a similar product already?

2 - Does the company have financial backing?

Many experts believe a company must have $12 million behind it just to get started, and I would tend to agree. With limited financial backing, the chances of a company going under are obviously increased. But the backing is also necessary in order to keep up with the industry's big players with things like marketing material, apps, a website, a quality back office, etc. It's far easier to market an opportunity when everything the company has is world class, and you also want your reps to feel as though they are with the best company. Having a collective belief that everyone in the organization is on a winning ticket is very powerful, but it also costs money!

3 - Does the company understand network marketing?

Donald Trump attempted to launch his own network marketing company several years ago. Despite having a wealth of traditional business knowledge, he was unsuccessful, because that means little in this game. I would personally feel safer choosing a company with which the founders/owners either have extensive field experience or at the very least have employed people who do. A duplicable system, training, and tools are also crucial. You can have the best product and the best CEO in the world, but if you don't have a fast, simple, easy-to-duplicate system in place, the company won't thrive.

4 - Business operations

Although it is crucial to have in-the-field network marketing experience, at the end of the day someone has to run the back end of the company. There is nothing worse than working with a company that has an incompetent or nonexistent customer care team or a commissions department that pays people incorrectly. So make sure that the company is operating proficiently behind the scenes too.

5 - The people

The people and culture within a company are the most important element of all. It doesn't matter how great the product, company, and system are, without good people and a supportive environment, the company probably won't last.

6 - The company is compliant

Having a DSA-approved company helps a lot. But this doesn't mean to say that all companies lacking DSA approval are bad. It is vital that your company understands network marketing and product laws in every country they are open in, otherwise they can fall apart as quickly as they are built. In my relatively short career I have seen several network marketing companies in my home country, Australia, have to stop operation completely because they didn't abide by national rules or regulations. The downside to following regulations: it's expensive and slow. But remember, Rome wasn't built in a day!

Ten Tips Before Starting

"Empty your cup so that it may be filled; become devoid to gain totality."
—*Bruce Lee*

Before starting, we need to make some mind-set shifts (if you want to get results fast). We need to "empty our cup" so that we can then refill it with the necessary information and belief systems to enable success. Network marketing is like *no other job or business in the world*. I learned the hard way that the network marketing game was vastly different to anything I had tried before. Like most of us, I came into the industry with plenty of skills from my various thirteen careers and thought my sales persuasion techniques and nutrition knowledge was going to change the game of network marketing. I refused to follow the existing system because none of it made sense to me, and I even called it "amateur" and "backward." This mentality caused me a lot of failure, a lot of frustration, and a lot of wasted time. I soon learned that open-mindedness and a strong commitment are two traits we need in order to make this journey as successful as possible. I will expand on these details as we go, but I need you to help me help you! So let's get into it.

1) I need you to believe in the industry.

The first person you need to sell is yourself. This is most effectively achieved by believing in what the experts are saying as opposed to your broke and negative friends and family. There are two decisions you will make in your network marketing career: the day that you decide to start and the day that you decide to truly commit yourself. I highly recommend making the second decision at the same time as you make the first. You will have a million questions, fears, and doubts, but that is all normal. You need to look at the history of this industry and understand that it is one of the biggest industries in the world that has stood the test of time and created tens of thousands of millionaires. Yes, that's right, tens of thousands of millionaires. It is being endorsed by almost every business expert, author, and economist on the planet. Those cold, hard facts should be enough to sink any doubts. Have faith. If you don't believe, read the endorsements ten times over until you have certainty, because until you are sold, you are going to find it very difficult to influence others.

2) I need you to believe in you.

Your opinion of yourself becomes your reality. If you have self-doubt, you cannot expect anyone else to believe in your vision, and you won't get very far. On the other hand, if you think the opposite and do believe in yourself, you've taken the first step in making your dreams a reality. Sometimes it can be good to remind yourself that this industry has already produced tens of thousands of millionaires, and the good news is that none of these people were born network marketers. They were not necessarily well edu-cated, nor did they come from a wealthy background, and they aren't six foot six and beautiful either! They are everyday people who started out with average skills and an average mind-set but believed in themselves and the journey to stick it out long enough to become successful. We all have our own unique strengths and talents, so find them and use them. As a result of the negativity, doubt, and fear that society has programmed into most of us, you might be thinking, "Dave, I have no skills—I'm awful." But know that deep down, below that fear lies a giant, waiting to be woken. And one of the best things about this industry is that you are going to have a long line of people with a financial interest in you to help get you out of your shell and shine. Remember "every master was once a disaster." All of the basic required skills are learnable through practice and preparation, creating the confidence we certainly don't start with. To touch briefly on what will be discussed in a later chapter, you need to start visualizing yourself as being successful, and the next step is to work on making that a reality. I was terrified of public speaking, but I visualized and rehearsed it in my head thousands of times. Now they can't shut me up!

3) I need you to commit for as long as you would for a university degree (two to four years).

Most people don't give anything a long enough chance to become successful at it. Look at gym memberships, for example. Most gyms that have five thousand members are lucky to have one thousand of those active because if we don't get immediate results, we stop. You need to change these habits if you want success in this business or any area of life for that matter. Nothing comes easy; you aren't entitled to anything; and you will only get out what you put in. Most people spend thousands of dollars and four years of their life studying at a university. They master a profession that will earn them barely enough money to get by in the New Era economy (if they get a job at all), yet when they are introduced to an industry that can provide the wealth for them to live out every dream and desire they ever had, they only give themselves a couple of months to master it. If people had to spend $50,000 and commit to four years of learning the business, I think network marketing would be a multimillionaire machine! So make the commitment that you will still be here in two years. At the end of the day, you are still going to be working anyway, so why not have a no-risk shot at creating your dreams, learning some amazing skills, and building an endless network along the way?

To put it simply: don't quit, don't jump between down-lines, and don't jump between companies.

4) Go pro!

As network marketing author and guru Eric Worre's book title suggests, if you're going to do network marketing, you might as well *Go Pro*! And that's the same with everything in life; there is no point in doing anything half-hearted. If we go to the gym with that approach, then we won't have a program or a goal, and we won't commit the necessary time. So what do we get? Terrible results! But when we treat our program like an athlete, set goals, and track our progress, what do we get? We change our lives. So I urge you to do the same with this industry. You will never reach your dreams if you do it halfheartedly, so decide to become a professional. I promise you that it will be worthwhile.

5) Unlearn.

Most of the skills that you acquired in other industries need to be thrown in the bin. You may have been the best real estate agent in the country—congratulations, but it doesn't work here. You may be an NLP master sales persuasion trainer who filled rooms—again, congratulations. I am sure that you can close more car sales than any other salesperson at the yard, but throw it out because it doesn't work here. At the university you were taught to rotely learn information so you could recite it for exams. But again this won't work for duplicating reps. We will cover this in detail shortly. So forget what you know because to be successful in this business, you first need to "empty the cup."

6) Ditch the negative baggage around success and money.

The people who say that money isn't important usually don't have any. Most often they tried to make their fortune, but it didn't work out, and now they're bitter about the whole subject. To put it simply, it's a loser's mentality. They failed at the money game, so now they claim it's unimportant. They say they don't need money to be happy, but at the same time they're going gray from stress; they're anxious, working three jobs, and crying themselves to sleep! And I'm speaking from personal experience here. If you say that money is not important, do you think you will ever get any? Of course you won't. So when the next person tells you that he or she doesn't need money, grab a computer, log on to that person's online bank account and get that individual to transfer his or her money to you! The pursuit of wealth is not evil; in fact, it's noble, and it's definitely not spiritual to be poor. I believe that a lack of money is the cause of most of the world's problems today. You don't see billionaires like Bill Gates robbing banks, stealing and lying, or entering into prostitution or extortion. I don't see him draining taxpayer money for his unemployment payments. No, I see him donating billions of dollars to charity and to people in need around the world every year. The financial freedom that can be achieved in network marketing liberates people from money slavery. Just like the lyrics to The Verve's *Bittersweet Symphony,* "You're a slave to the money, then you die." Sadly, it's a true story for most. If you earn just enough money for the necessities to survive, you're a slave to the dollar. Being poor has never helped a single starving child or contributed to finding cures for disease. So let's get comfortable with the idea of pursuing and achieving wealth. It's the greatest thing that you can do for yourself, your family, and society. Remember, money doesn't make you good or bad, it just magnifies what you are already. What I can say from personal experience is that I've seen people become a lot happier and less stressed without money issues. I've been broke, and I've been on a pretty sizable annual income, and I highly recommend the latter.

7) Listen to your up-line.

You are going to jump into this opportunity full of excitement and ideas. You are going to think of a million and one shortcuts to fast track the building of your organization. These usually range from mass letter box drops to blogs, websites, spam e-mails, boot camps, and even to buying a shop and retailing the product. The list of ideas will be endless, and you will question the system that the company uses and probably (like me) think that you know more than everyone else. I can tell you now that every idea you think of has been thoroughly tested and exhausted countless times already. Network marketing has some of the smartest business minds on the planet developing its system. Its methods are not always traditional, but they have built one of the largest industries in the world. I personally don't like to kill people's creativity because using our skills and expanding our minds is one of the main reasons why we jump into a business like this. I developed my own strategy for incorporating new ideas: put 5 percent of your effort into your own ideas and concepts and put 95 percent of your effort into what has been proven to work.

8) Keep your eye on the prize and avoid getting caught in the details.

Now I am certainly not saying that you don't want to eventually understand the finer details of the industry and company that you work with, but if you wait to figure it all out before you start, you will probably never start at all. Far too often people get stuck in "paralysis by analysis" as a way of stalling due to fear. It's really quite simple. You find customers like every other business in the world, and you find other people who also want to sell the product, like every business or franchise in the world. Your company will have an above-average product because without it they would never have launched and probably wouldn't be around today. So don't get stuck in the details; instead, focus on a big vision and results. At the end of the day, it's all people really care about. I have no idea how my mobile phone allows me to speak to another person on the opposite side of the planet. All I know is that I pay my bills, and I get to speak to my closest friends whenever I want—no matter where they are. I get the result

I'm after. If you wait until you know everything before getting started, you will probably die before your business hits momentum.

9) If you don't have naysayers, you probably don't have success either.

No matter what new venture you decide to pursue, you are guaranteed to meet a certain amount of negativity and even violent opposition from everyday people living in mediocrity, and there are a number of reasons why. Firsy, it's easier to pull people down than to lift them up. They say that 95 percent of all human thoughts are negative, and the number of people living in victimhood and infected with mind viruses is alarming. Second, your desire to better yourself, your pursuit of a new business, and your newfound hunger for self-development challenges their belief systems and shakes the foundations of their world. And third, every inch of your success will highlight their failure and missed opportunities. So understand that when you have haters, critics, and naysayers, you should smile, because it's a universal sign that you are on the right track. When they start talking behind your back, you should know it's a by-product of success because they only talk about the successful ones! Ninety-nine percent of the negativity these people create is in their minds. People will constantly create drama and scenarios that aren't actually factual. They are in FEAR: false evidence appearing real. Some of the people closest to you will be negative. Half will not want you to succeed because it highlights their failures, as I mentioned previously, and the other half will have the best intentions for you, but they are stuck in a world of fear as a result of their mind viruses and negative programming. At one point or another you will get someone violently opposed to what you do, and this is the point where you will have to decide whether you take the advice of someone whose life you don't want to be living (the biggest critics always seem to be the most broke) or the advice of the wealthiest people on the planet who have a proven track record. It's a no-brainer, and I'm pretty sure that you are big enough and strong enough to figure this one out. But you can't let the naysayers get to you. Avoid arguments with stupid people because they will bring you down to their level and beat you every time. Not everyone can be saved; not everyone can be helped, but don't let someone else's fears and insecurities kill your dreams—*ever*!

Remember, it's easy to sit back in the crowd and criticize or "hate" on people. It's something that requires no skill, talent, or heart, and these spectators of life are stuck in the grandstand, never to experience success in the game of life.

10) Your inner world creates your outer world.

Whatever you believe will become your reality (your beliefs become true for you), and your results are determined by your thoughts, not by your circumstances. As I discussed in the opening chapters, your outer world is truly a reflection of your inner world. This may sound crazy, I know, and we will discuss it further in later chapters, but what you must understand is that what you subconsciously believe about the industry is passed on to your prospects, and any limiting beliefs you have will be reflected in their response. So before you say, "Oh those people won't be interested," remember that most people will be highly interested in an opportunity to make money. You just need to get better at articulating your message. Understand that every single person would get started if he or she believed that he or she could have the results that network marketing can provide.

Dream Building

"If you can dream it, you can do it." —Walt Disney

The possibilities in network marketing are enormous, so I want you to start dreaming. Give yourself permission to get excited about life again, perhaps for the first time since you were a child. Before I had everything I have today, I visualized my future in great detail—thousands of times, night after night. I visualized doing business with my best friends, our successes together, the overseas trips, the good times. I visualized the cars, the big events, the lifestyle, and the person I am becoming today. I even visualized writing this book and had a detailed description of the partner I intended on meeting. I found the visualization process to be somewhat euphoric; after all, what could be better than seeing every one of my dreams as a reality? The greatest times in my life to that point in time had been playing sports as a kid. I played in a lot of successful teams, and winning with my best friends was like the ultimate high. It was better than any movie, song, drug, or potion in the world. So my drive wasn't only selfish; my vision was of a successful army of people who all enjoyed success together. But this time we weren't playing for a plastic trophy. We were playing to win the game of life.

The reason why I now believe so strongly in the power of the human mind is because, believe it or not, all of the things I visualized in great detail when starting out on this journey have actually come true. Even my personal relationships (including the one with my partner) were affirmed on paper, visualized, and manifested into the reality I experience today. The power of the human mind and imagination is still beyond my belief. But what I do know is that it has some effect, so I continue to do it!

We all have different values and driving forces. For some people it's family, and for others it's about the ability to travel and work with others. Whatever your highest values in life may be, you need two things to be able to incorporate them into your life: time and money! This is what makes network marketing the ultimate dream-building vehicle because it can provide you with endless amounts of both of these things.

To turn your dreams and desires into a tangible reality, you need to be able to do the following:

- See it
- Believe it (use your senses)
- Articulate it
- Take action on it

I believe these are the four necessary steps to achieving any dream or goal.

You must first learn to see and believe in your dreams as fervently as if they were already a reality. Then all you must do is bide the time for them to manifest. By the way, this isn't new information. You can read about it in *Think and Grow Rich* by Napoleon Hill or in Rhonda Byrne's book, *The Secret*. My vision was so vivid that my future existed like a tangible island to me. It was so close, and I could see it so clearly. All I had to do was sail over and step ashore. When you reach this level of belief, your intentions are sent out to the universe via your thoughts, by way of the conviction in your speech, and through your body language. And when you are certain enough, the universe will conspire to help you achieve your every desire. This makes a lot more sense when you understand that our universe is made up of energy, and the "solid" three-dimensional reality we experience on a daily basis is nothing more than energy vibrating at a low frequency. But essentially all you need to know is that you are truly the architect of your own world. A painter puts his or her brush to canvas each day and over time creates his or her masterpiece. An entrepreneur does the same thing, but instead of a paintbrush he or she harnesses the incredible power of the human mind with affirmations and visualizations, and slowly but surely what was once just a thought begins to manifest into physical reality. Matthew McConaughey's 2014 Oscar speech hit the nail on the head when he spoke about chasing the person he was going to be a year from now. That is visualizing and belief at its best.

But even having a clear dream and believing in it deeply isn't enough. In this industry we rely on others to be successful as well, so they must also believe and see the vision. You must learn to paint a picture with words because they have a powerful effect. One of the strengths I had when getting started was the ability to incorporate team success with my own personal goals. This meant that it wasn't all about me and made it easy to pique the interest of others. Also remember that most people don't have the confidence or belief in themselves to dream, so when you can do it for them, it's very powerful. I believe that the secret behind a powerful *why*, or helping to rebuild someone's dreams again, is making the dream bigger than just one's self and including team success. Because the only thing better than achieving success yourself is enjoying it with the people you love.

Last and most importantly, we must take action on that dream. Keep in mind that taking action becomes very simple once you are already able to see it, believe it, and articulate it. Once you reach this level, you will begin to experience life from a whole new perspective. The days of sleeping in will be over, replaced instead with a sense of excitement and purpose. Your ambitions will override any fear that once existed, and you will go and get the job done.

Will You Take the Blue Pill or the Red Pill?

I love the classic scene in the *Matrix* in which Neo is confronted with the difficult choice of going back to what he has always known or discovering the truth of his existence. He must decide whether to take the blue pill and return to his life as a computer programmer—and forget he ever found out the "truth"—or take the red pill and discover how deep the rabbit hole goes. I believe that this is representative of a dilemma we all face in our lives when we are met with adversity. The path most traveled is to follow in the footsteps of our parents and go to school, then load ourselves up with debt at university, get into even more debt with a mortgage, and find a corporate job with the hope that they pay us well and keep us until retirement. Or instead we can choose to be great. We can take life's challenges as they come and chase down our dreams. I think everybody would agree that no child has ever dreamed of becoming an office worker who just gets by on an average income. But there is a point in our lives when we decide to settle for less—far less—than what our dreams had in store for us. I have lived the equivalent of both the red pill and the blue pill, and I highly recommend the red pill. Take my word for it; don't settle for anything less than your dreams. I know what it's like to have no money, and I know what it's like to have a reasonable amount, and I highly recommend the latter. *Success may appear more difficult at times, but a life of financial struggle, mediocrity, and desperation is far more difficult in the long run.*

Exercise #1:
Use power questions to visualize your dreams. Do the following exercise and imagine yourself in five and ten years' time.

Where do you live?
Who do you surround yourself with?
Where do you travel?
What are you known and admired for?
What impact have you made on others?
What do you earn?
What do you drive?

Exercise #2:

Take time each day to visualize your goals for not only the year but the rest of your life. I believe that this technique is most effective when you are at a high vibration. Some people use music or exercise; others play with their pet. It doesn't really matter—just as long as you are feeling great!

Exercise #3:

Your dream life has a financial figure attached to it, and the reality is that we live in a world where our options are controlled by money. Your dream-life number is what you need to earn residually in order to live however you wish. I say residually because most people's ultimate dream lives don't include going to work.

Attach the weekly cost beside each of the following to develop your dream life number:

Dream income number per week
Dream home
Holiday home/s
Holiday costs
Car/cost
Dining cost
Electricity/phone/cable TV/Internet
Cleaner/landscaper, etc.
Clothing
Charity
Family
Children/tuition

Other lifestyle activities
Savings
Investments
Education
Other

Starting Fast with Six Steps

"If you can't explain it simply, you don't understand it well enough."

—ALBERT EINSTEIN

THROUGHOUT MY CAREER I BEGAN TO ADOPT THE PHILOSOPHY that it's better to slowly build a house of bricks that lasts forever than to quickly build a house of straw that doesn't last long. There is certainly some truth to this; however, I learned the hard way that this isn't entirely true when getting people started in network marketing.

In this business we want to build a house of bricks, but we also want to build it quickly. When you build too slowly there is more room for error in duplication and an extended time in which the new rep isn't getting paid, which increases the likelihood of him or her dropping off. In my organization I had some really sharp people on board, so we got away with building it slowly for a certain period of time. However, we eventually hit a lid and got stuck at a certain depth. It wasn't until we stepped back and evaluated what the fastest-growing companies were doing (and what we weren't doing) that we discovered the power of getting started quickly.

Now I am sure that your company has a fast-start process already in place—mine did also. My advice is to stick to it; don't try to outsmart a proven system. We found that by following a simple fast-start system, new reps were able to lock down a greater number of meetings. But when the duplication process was slower, they had more time to become "experts" on the topic, and their guest count began to dry up. How could we possibly know more and get a lesser result? Well, when new reps know too much too soon, they talk too much to their prospects and, as I like to put it, "spoil the movie."

The fast-start training needs to be so short and fast that it can be done following a presentation to get people trained on the spot. The key requirements are setting goals, developing a contact list, and learning how to effectively invite prospects to a presentation. All of the other advanced stuff can be learned along the way because you need people making money quickly, especially when working with Gen Y, who can't concentrate or stick to anything for longer than a couple of minutes (I get to make fun of Gen Ys because I am one). If you want the fast growth that the top companies are getting each year, this is what you need to do and how you need to operate. Might it be outside of your comfort zone? Yes, just like everything is at the beginning. But adapt, figure it out, and get people hosting their first meetings as soon as possible.

Step One: Start with *Why*

"When the why is big enough, the details, problems and 'how to' take care of themselves." —Dave Nelson

One of the best business books of the last decade is Simon Sinek's *Start with Why*. It's an approach that focuses on what matters. And what matters is not the *what* nor the *how* but the *why*. Sinek explains how some of the powerhouse companies like Apple have thrived because of a core understanding of the reason for why they do what they do. If you read Steve Jobs's autobiography, you will see what drove him to be one of the greatest visionaries and entrepreneurs in history. It wasn't because of his skill; it was the legacy he wanted to leave and the movement he wanted to make across the world to change the way we do just about everything. You have to understand that people will move mountains when they are aligned with a *why* that incorporates their highest values and goals. The vast majority of people go through their lives completely disconnected from a great purpose. These people don't have goals; they have given up on their dreams, and it's your job to set out their *why* (goals, values, dreams) early on—to remind them of what is possible.

Your *why* is going to play two main roles for you.

First, it's going to drive you. It's going to get you out of bed with excitement each morning and help to get you through the tough times as they inevitably arise, and it's also going to play an integral role in what you visualize, believe, and eventually achieve. Your *why* power is 150 times stronger than your willpower. Therefore, you need to make it big. The bigger it is, the more influence over your daily decisions it will have, and you will say no to things that no longer serve you and your highest purpose. So please don't just breeze through building your *why* because it has the power to strongly influence the direction of your future. Take it seriously, and I promise you that this vehicle will help you get anywhere you wish.

Second, your *why* is going to have an impact on others, so we need to work on your ability to share it well. It's going to break down walls that others have constructed to protect themselves when talking about the opportunity. We have all heard the John C. Maxwell saying, "Nobody cares what you know until they know how much you care." The saying is especially true for this industry. People are naturally skeptical of what your intention is when you approach them with an opportunity. So your *why* is designed to clearly make your intention known and to take down their barriers before going into any details. Your *why* should create likability, love, trust, and a "me too" response from the audience. Remember that facts tell, but stories sell! Your *why* is your life story, your business mission, and the cause that people are going to buy into. The bigger and clearer it is, the more committed and passionate your new team members will be.

The *why* is effective for:

> Motivating your internal drive
> Inviting people
> Presenting
> Getting people started

So as you can see, your story must be conducive to sharing—not in the same way as acting out a Shakespeare play but as if you were having a meaningful conversion with someone.

Your *why* should be structured something like this:

1) Where you were:

Focus on frustrations that you had in your life. The more universal your frustrations are (lack of money and energy, for example) the wider your audience appeal will be. Simply explaining how once upon a time you were broke won't cut it. Instead you need to tell the story of what it was like to be broke and, most importantly, how it made you feel. Tell a particular story that best represents that time when you were so hard-pressed for money, and if you want to be authentic, talk about the emotions you felt when you were struggling. The particular details of your circumstances don't matter, but the emotions do. You will be amazed by how many people can relate to an honest account of your experiences.

2) What you saw:

Talk about the things you liked most about the business opportunity when you were initially presented with it. Again, tell some stories here. What were some things that inspired you? Did you know someone who changed his or her life around? Telling stories like this builds credibility, generates trust, and creates social proof.

3) Vision:

You should always finish your *why* by talking about where you are now and the vision you have for yourself and, more importantly, the team. It's no good to just talk about what you want to achieve for yourself. Only someone with team success in mind is a true leader who should be followed. So make your intention clear that you are interested in the success of your team members because ultimately they are buying into the team!

Imagine that you are the manager of your favorite sporting team, and you want to get the best player in the league to join you. Wouldn't you need to share a vision with this player to give him or her an idea of where the team is going and what he or she could achieve with you? Essentially the same principles apply in network marketing. You're the manager of your very own Manchester United or LA Lakers, and you've got to draw in the talent.

Tip: A good *why* will tap into both pleasure and pain. Remember that some people are driven by the pain and frustrations in their life, while others are goal and vision oriented. So if you include universal frustrations as well as a big vision, you have a great combination.

Where you were (pain)
What you saw (testimonials)
Where you are going (pleasure)

Remember not to just talk about your own personal success; you will need a team vision and a cause that's greater than yourself. Let's be honest, no one is going to want to work his or her tail off to pay for your Ferrari. Far too many people get stuck in their own *why* and goals and want to tell everyone about them, but really—no one cares. If you give off the vibe that new reps are just being recruited to build your dream, I can promise you that they won't come in with a whole lot of passion—if they join you at all.

If you genuinely have a great and noble cause—one that is about making positive change and challenges the norm—you are going to have a much easier time making it stick and getting commitment. Be vulnerable sharing your *why* because people don't want to see scripted presentations anymore. We are dying for emotion and truth and for someone to tell it like it is. If you want to start a revolution, be that person!

Step Two: The List

"The best real estate agents always have new listings, and the best network marketers are always adding people to their list." —Dave Nelson

Your list is arguably the most important element of your business, yet most new reps never write one. While your ability to start a big list is crucial, your ability to continually build a list week in and week out will put you in the top 1 percent of network marketers. The most successful reps in my organization have an infectious personality; they speak to everyone; and by the end of each week, they end up with at least five to ten new relationships. They may not pitch to every one of them, but when the time and place is right, it can be very effective.

When starting your list, write down *everyone* you know. This includes Facebook friends, phone contacts, e-mail contacts—the works. For some people this is an enormous list, and if so, great! This industry will pay you for the network you have built over the years. Now writing every person we know down does not mean that we are going to pitch to all of them, but at the very least we will most likely approach most of them about our product.

But regardless of this, get all of the names down on paper. Even if it's not for them, they may refer you to people they know who are interested. I have several stories in which the prospect wasn't interested but was more than happy to set us up for a meeting with a friend of his or hers that this individual knew would be perfect for it. According to the rule of six degrees of separation, everyone on the planet is connected through six people. Well this industry is somewhat built on that formula.

List Tracking

Having a list is also crucial for tracking prospects. See it as relationship management, where you can monitor and keep the relationship with people you are speaking to.

List Building

If you have studied the art of making money online, you will know that the fortune is in your list. In network marketing it's very similar, and we need to be continually adding to it. When you get a business card, put the name on the list; when you chat with someone on Facebook, add him or her to your list. Every new person you meet on a daily basis should be added to your list. Now this doesn't mean that we are going to go spamming them with e-mails and text messages. Instead, regularly reviewing the list will allow us to make tactful contact once we see that he or she is suitable. It's as simple as building rapport, sending a tool, and then planning to have a meeting and partnership. Remember that most sales occur after three to eight points of seeing the product or service. So if you are speaking to as many people as you should be, it would be impossible to track those numbers without a manageable list.

Step Three: The Invitation

"You can have the greatest opportunity in the world, but it's useless if no one sees it." —Dave Nelson

The goal of your invitation is to get the prospect (warm or cold) to come see a presentation. It is *not* to present the opportunity (over the phone or via text or e-mail). New reps are often full of excitement and ideas, and they want to run off and tell everyone they know about the business. We call this "ignorance on fire," and it can work in rare instances, but for most it will burn their warm contacts, and they will have to wait two to three months before they can reapproach them. This is not the ideal start.

Let's take a look at some different invitation scenarios. At the end of the day, they all have the same goal: get the prospect to view a tool (a tool is normally a video, audio, or magazine article) and to attend a presentation. Why use a tool? Why not just get them to the meeting? Well as good as that sounds, the reality is that *all* reps end up talking too much, and they "spoil the movie." Would you be as inclined to see a movie if you already knew the whole plot? Probably not, and it's the same with the opportunity. Once a prospect feels that he or she knows it all, that person is no longer intrigued and often becomes dismissive. Also, the majority of reps that come into the business will not have enough influence among their friends to get them to a meeting. The tool creates leverage for new people who don't know how to explain it all yet and prevents them from saying too much before they know what they are talking about. As you become more advanced, you won't want to waste your time at meetings with prospects that aren't interested. There's nothing worse than doing a meeting with someone who was dragged there, has no idea why, and has no interest in doing the business. The tool should qualify your prospects and sort the interested from the uninterested, speeding up the entire process. And if they aren't interested in the information in the tool, then of course we don't want to waste their time or ours by taking them to a presentation.

What tool do I use? Well it depends on your company's system. If they have a tool created for you in video, audio, or written format, use it. If they don't, then that's fine also. There are plenty of generic industry tools that are great for piquing interest. For business-minded prospects you can look at audios like *Escape the Rat Race* by Randy Gage, and there's also *The Next Millionaire* or any video on YouTube by Paul Zane Pilzer. Donald Trump and Robert Kiyosaki also have a great PDF available on Google called *Why we Recommend Network Marketing,* and there are plenty of other options too. But the key reason behind why these tools are so effective is the caliber of the people who are endorsing the industry. Having some of the wealthiest people on the planet endorse the opportunity to your prospect helps to lay the foundation for an effective face-to-face meeting. The tool also lets brand-new reps be able to bring in business on day one, even when they know little to nothing about how it works! In fact, time and time again I have seen reps execute their most effective invitations within their first week of business. Why? Because the rep doesn't know enough to be able to say too much, and he or she is generally quite nervous and wants to get off the phone quickly.

So let's look at some different scenarios that reps will face when inviting. Remember that these are just guidelines. I don't believe there is a cookie-cutter one-invitation-fits-all solution.

I like to break down the invitations into three sections: cold, warm direct, and warm passive. I personally like the direct approach when talking to my warm market, but I also understand that not everyone has the confidence to talk to their friends and family like that, and often people have fear around the idea of selling to friends. So this is where the passive, no-pressure invitation comes into play. It's comfortable yet still very effective for all types of people.

The key thing to remember when talking to your warm market is to talk to them like you normally would. Far too many people turn on their business mode and start talking like a salesperson. The aggressive direct approach is suited to people that you know are business minded or who have a drive for making money.

Warm Market Direct

- Greet as per usual.
- Tell a genuine story of what results you saw and lived.
- Promote the viewing of a tool (audio, video or article).
- Confirm party time.

For example: (Name), I actually wanted to talk to you about a new project that I've just gotten started with. A good friend of mine has been involved for a couple of months now and... (insert truthful success story of either product or opportunity). So I'm having a launch party, and he is actually coming over to help me out with the process. I've invited a few select people to come around to discuss my new project on (insert date) this week, and I really think if we teamed up on this thing we could do big things together!

If he or she asks for more information, is resistant, *or* says yes, we use the tool. Use the tool no matter what!

Okay, I'm going to send you a short video that gives you a brief overview of it all.

Here is where you promote the tool. Send whichever tool you think will pique his or her interest most effectively. For example, I might have a business-minded prospect that I may decide to send the YouTube link to the "Cash Flow Quadrant" by Robert Kiyosaki. If so, I would say:

This video is by the most successful business and wealth-creation author of all time, and he talks about the best way for the average person to create wealth. This is life-changing info, and I think we can capitalize on what he is talking about.

Can you make sure you watch it before you come?

[Response]

Great; I look forward to seeing you (insert date). I think it's going to be a lot of fun, and there are going to be some great people there, so I'm sure it will be worth your time.

Warm Market Passive

- Greet as per usual.
- Build genuine rapport as usual.

For example: (Name), the reason I called is because I've been working on a side project, and this week I'm actually having a launch party at my place. I would love to have you there. It's going to be a lot of fun. There will be products that we offer there, of course, and I'm looking for business partners too, which is what I really want you to check out. If you're not interested, that's fine, but I need to fill the room and would really appreciate some support from my friends and family. So it would be great to have you there.

If you have a house party:

I'm actually having two launches. One is on (insert date) and the other on (insert date). Do either one of those work well for you?

If you want to see that person one-on-one or if he or she can't make the party:

Well, why don't we catch up for coffee? I'll show you how it all works, and it may or may not be for you; either way it would be great to catch up. It's been way too long!

[Response]

Awesome! Well, before we catch up, let me send you some information on it all so that you'll know a little more about it. (Promote the tool.)

Cold Market

When talking to cold prospects, realize that the faster they become your warm market, the easier the invitation becomes. So the ability to generate good rapport is a crucial skill for any network marketer. Remember, if you can master this very basic skill of cold marketing, you will always have new business for the rest of your career, and you will set yourself up to be one of the best in the industry. If you're going to see a person regularly, like the receptionist at your gym, you don't need to pitch to him or her the first time you chat. Build the relationship, create some intrigue behind what you do, and wait for the time to be right. Or even better, wait for that person to ask what it is that you do. This is another example of how when you want to limit the amount of talking you do, use an appropriate tool instead. I like to accompany the tool with a genuine compliment. No one compliments each other these days, and it's likely to increase his or her probability of viewing the tool.

Example:

-Build massive rapport.
-Ask lots of questions and smile, smile, smile! (People are attracted to enthusiastic happy people, not serious and awkward ones.)

Always pitch as you are leaving:

I have to run now, but I run a business from home, and I'm actually looking for partners at the moment. And from what I've seen and heard from you already, I think you would be fantastic and could do really well. I haven't got time to go through it right now, but can I send you some info on the business to review?

[Response]

Okay, great. Well, check it out, and I'll touch base with you at (insert time), and you can let me know if you're a yay or a nay. But if you're interested, let's set up a time to have coffee and discuss it further.

In my opinion, any invitation technique can work as long as you are confident, happy, and radiate enthusiastic energy. This is why I believe that there isn't one perfect invitation technique that will suit everyone. If you feel comfortable with the approach, so will the prospect. So my advice is to use whatever feels like "you." I also like the technique of finding out what the other person wants. This approach is always easy as you're simply offering them a solution to what they want. You can use simple power questions like the following:

Have you thought about working from home before?
Are you interested in creating multiple sources of income?
Have you thought about running your own business?
If I could show you a way to (insert their goals) would you be interested?

(The last question is the one that was used to effectively prospect me when I was working on the cruise ship.)

These are all generally "yes" questions, which can lead us to sending that individual a tool or providing details of how we can achieve whatever it is that he or she wants.

Tools Create Duplication and Results

If your system requires new reps to train until they are proficient enough to lock down meetings, your business won't grow exponentially. Your organization will hit a lid, and only the talented reps will produce. The tool creates duplication and gives everyday people without influence over their friends a legitimate chance of having success. And the secret to exponential growth in network marketing isn't getting your top 20 percent to produce (because they always will); it's about making sure the bottom 80 percent are doing something, getting paid, and enjoying their experience with the company.

Product or Opportunity Lead?

This really depends on whether you want the prospect to be a customer or an independent representative. If you think this person is suited to network marketing, always lead with the opportunity, and you can then down-sell to the products later. Understand that if you lead with the product but you want to build the business, it's going to be a slower process. Having said this, if you're with a direct sales company, leading with the product first has proven itself to be effective. So again, whatever feels most comfortable to you will probably work best, and whatever you feel awkward with, won't. It's much easier to start high and then downgrade than it is to do it the other way around. One thing I would recommend is to not fall into the trap of having a team with no customers. Imagine having one hundred McDonald's franchises with no customers—it wouldn't work either. But also know that if you only have customers—just like if there were only one McDonald's store in the world—your income capacity will have a lid on it. So to summarize, it's really both. You need both, so approach both accordingly.

Anticipation Is the Magic

If you can speak in a way that builds anticipation (think of a movie trailer), you will have much better retention to your presentations. So like a movie trailer, don't say too much in your invitation and don't give away too much detail. Use EGCUP (excited, genuine, certain, urgent, and passionate) in your language to achieve this. If you can combine EGCUP and link the business as a way to achieve their goals, you should have a good attendance ratio and avoid no-shows. At the end of the day, if prospects think that attending a presentation can get them the things they want in life and they see you excited about it, they will generally show up.

Remember that this is relationship marketing, not sales. Eighty percent of signups occur within the third to eighth point of contact, so a typical signup may even take as long as this:

- Send the prospect an invitation that involves viewing a tool,
- He or she comes to a house presentation.
- A one-on-one meeting comes next.
- The prospect comes to a big city presentation.
- He or she is taken through the sign-up process and then trained.

So if these statistics are true, which I believe they are, the fortune really is in the follow-up. The invitation is really just the first of many points of contact in the relationship.

MILLION-DOLLAR TIP:
Asking the prospect what he or she wants rather than telling him or her what you have is the easiest and most effective technique, yet it's rarely used.

Step Four: The Presentation

"The key to presenting in the New Era is to not present at all." —Dave Nelson

The idea of presenting was one of the key factors behind my initial excitement to join the network marketing industry. It was something I feared but at the same time always wanted to learn, and I practiced enough to become quite good at it. I would watch endless YouTube clips of my favorite speakers, break down their talks, analyze their body language and tonality, and scrutinize their speech. I did everything I could to become the best presenter. I found it easy to create laughs, own the crowd, use highs and lows in my tone, and create intrigue. I used all the tricks in the book to make my presentations engaging, funny, aggressive, and paradigm-shaking. And although it worked very well for the aggressive types, I soon realized that my sign-up ratio was incredibly low. My presentations weren't quite as good as I thought they were. I later discovered that my effort to master presenting was not duplicable. Whatever your prospects see you do will be what they believe is expected of them. So when I was up on stage aggressively listing endless numbers of useless statistics, what I was doing to most of the audience was creating a feeling of "I could never do that." To increase my sign-up ratio, I instead needed to generate an overwhelming feeling of "wow, I can do that."

Regardless of whether the presentation is in front of one or one hundred people, it needs to be so simple that others think they could do it too. This is why "press play" presentations have become so popular. Companies have realized that a video is the ultimate "I can do that" creator. However, at big-venue presentations, even if your company has a "press play" video, I always believe in using the human element, and the respected leader should speak for a longer period.

I see the presentation as being made up of three key parts, and ineffectiveness in any of those parts will ruin the whole presentation.

The presentation should run in this order:

1) Why
2) What
3) How to

Why:

As we discussed earlier, the *why* is the most important element of the presentation because it builds rapport with the prospects. At a presentation your goal is to connect with the audience, and this means being real and raw—people don't want to feel like you're reading a script to them. But I believe that the most important objective of the presentation is to uncover the *why* of each person in the audience. Nobody dream-builds these days, so you want to capture their vision and their values and attach them to the business. If the *why* is big enough and people believe that they can achieve their dreams through this platform, then 99 percent of the job is already done!

Here are some example questions that will get the audience visualizing their future:

Where do you want to be in five years' time? What does your life look like in a perfect world? How much do you work? What do you earn? What do you drive? Where do you travel? What do people say about you?

Here's the secret to creating their *why*: it needs a dollar value. Whatever the personal circumstances of their *why* may be, they will always need a certain amount of money and a lot of time freedom to make it a reality. So the key is to make a very clear point of the fact that their current plan (generally working a job) will not get them to their necessary income. Getting this point across to the prospect will enhance the chances of creating an instant awakening by tenfold.

What:

The *what* is actually the least important part of the presentation but the area most people spend the most time on. Essentially it's an overview of the company and the opportunity. It needs to briefly cover the product, industry, and the company (in that order). Some facts are important, but remember that people are more worried about the results than the details (facts tell; stories sell). To use the same example as earlier, I have no idea how my mobile phone allows me to have a conversation with someone on the other side of the world. But I don't care either, nor do I need to know the details and science behind it. All I need to know is that if I pay my bills and dial in the number, I will get the desired result. Now if you can nail the perfect detailed and complex presentation, will it work? And will it even be more effective at times? Absolutely. But the question is, will it duplicate? And I can assure you that the answer is no! So if you want to create a full-time job for yourself and be required to do every presentation, be my guest. But remember, high-tech equals no check!

How:

The *how* is a vital part of the presentation. If the dream is built, the prospects are excited, and all of the facts and figures add up but they can't see *how* it's done, then they won't get started. They will have more questions, hesitate, and possibly even lose interest. The fastest-growing companies today are doing a fast-start training to finish the presentation. This involves a very brief overview of *how* to get started in the business. It's brilliant because if the fast-start system is simple and easy to follow, then people will feel that they can do it. And from my experience, when people have clarity, they gain confidence; the confidence soon leads to action.

House Presentations:

House presentations need to be a part of the weekly system because they are your money machines. The more house presentations you have set up in your organization each week, the more your income will grow. The $100 billion network marketing industry was built by using this method, and it has stood the test of time. In the New Era, the fastest-growing network marketing companies use them as their product volume driver. They work because they duplicate, and there are fewer unnecessary costs and less wasted time spent organizing. People feel more comfortable at someone's home, especially when they have already been there. The fastest-growing companies today are getting new reps to host their first house event within their first week. In my organization the teams who mastered the party or house presentation flew! Once you get a group of people together that are friends, that are having fun, and that are making money, you've got the magic formula! And because it's fun, social, and profitable, it duplicates too.

Venue/Hotel Presentations:
Hotel or venue presentations are important because they provide social proof, excitement, and camaraderie. So they are a mandatory part of a monthly system. But the question is how often should they run? We tried them once per week; we tried twice per week; and we tried fortnightly and eventually found that the best production came from a big presentation once a month in each major city. Now I know that experts all have their own opinions on this one, but in the New Era, people are busier than ever before, and having to commit to a weekly presentation on top of everything else becomes draining. People become bored quickly, and you can easily lose the excitement and energy that these meetings are meant to have. One thing was certain in my experience: when we changed from having a city presentation every week to having one every month, there was an instant increase in volume. Reps seemed more energetic, and the monthly presentations became huge. Figure it out for yourself, but I saw what happened in our organization, and I see what the top companies over the last few years have been doing, and they all stick to the once-per-month method.

The One-on-One:
Like house presentations and hotel presentations, one-on-one meetings are an important part of the exposure process. Often you will have contacts that you want to speak to in person before exposing them to a

presentation in a group environment. A one-on-one is also suitable following the presentation, to strategize and to go over any finer details that they may have questions about.

Webinar/Calls:
I also recommend having a weekly online presentation. As long as the reps in your organization don't become lazy and reliant on them, they can be extremely effective. Not only is this a great prospecting tool, but it's a great way for new reps to hear other stories and learn to present themselves.

Presentation Tips

Keep it simple.
We all want to do a "wow–factor" presentation, and although, yes, we should get that response, it can't be because of an advanced information overload. My presentations used to be like a tidal wave of all the information I knew, but this technique just left everyone confused and overwhelmed. I later learned the effectiveness of the KISS (keep it simple and sweet) principle. You also want to keep it relatively short. If you have sixty minutes of information, you are saying too much because there is no way that anyone can register that amount of information in one sitting.

Generate a "me too" and "I can do this" response.
We discussed this earlier, but it's a really important point. The more relaxed you are and the simpler the presentation, the better the energy of the meeting will be and the more positive the response from the audience will be.

Don't be a salesperson!
I mentioned this previously, but it's very important. In the New Era of sales, the key to presenting is to not present at all. We actually need to

"unpresent," if that is a word. People don't want to see you rock up with a suit and tie with your scripted PowerPoint pitch, trying to get them to say yes twenty-one times so they will buy. They want conversations; they want a no-BS raw discussion, and they want to see passion and enthusiasm. But it must be real! So the best advice you may ever get to nail a presentation is to be you, to tell it like it is, to be raw, and to be a good human being. Who would have thought it could be so simple?

Have fun!

A common mistake I see among new reps is becoming far too serious. Yes, of course it's natural to be a little nervous, but remember that it's only one of the many points of contact. The key is not to overload yourself with too much pressure to succeed. A tense rep with "serious eyes" and a stammering voice will make any prospect think, "I could never do this to my friends." So loosen up, have fun with it, smile, and don't act as if you're an expert when you're not because people will understand. As long as everyone is having fun, your duplication will increase, and people will be excited about hosting their own business launch nights.

Facts tell; stories sell.

Stories and testimonials are imperative. People want to see results, so the more stories and testimonials that you have as part of the presentation, the more likely people in the audience are to relate.

The setup:

If the setup is completed correctly, it doesn't matter how many mistakes are made during the presentation, it will still be effective. For example, I might be bringing a guest to a big presentation at which one of my top reps will be speaking. This rep is superaggressive and may offend some people, but I can soften the impact by the way I prepare my guest and set up the upcoming speaker. I can say to my prospect, "Look, this guy is really intense. It's just his style, but the great thing is that we use our own style and build our business in a way that suits us. So take the bits you like, and we will create our own master plan for you."

Closing:
It's a fact that most people are awful at closing. Some people can execute a world-class presentation, but they just can't quite finish it off cleanly by asking the magic words. My advice for this one is to come up with some lingo that you are comfortable saying. It's got to be something that you would say in a situation in which a decision must be made. For me it was something simple like, "So you wanna give this a crack?" or "Which set are you leaning toward?" However, I found the "one, two, three" method to be most effective as it provides the prospect with three options:

1. You just want to be a customer for the time being.
2. You want to be a customer and promote the products.
3. You want to be a customer, promote the products, and do the business.

My favorite lead question using this method is: "Which one are you leaning toward getting started with?" Then my next statement is: "On a scale of one to ten, one being not in a million years and ten being that you are ready to start now, where would you say you lie?" I like this method as it creates the clarity to create the next steps (such as a follow-up meeting or a training). Remember, the bigger the vision and clearer the plan, the less likely the prospect will be to worry or to question the price.

Now I fully understand that more often than not, we won't start people on the spot. In this scenario I still follow all of the steps of the training unless I get a firm "no." So, for example, I will be very assumptive and go through the fast-start training, even if they haven't gotten started yet. Often the training gives new or potential prospects the belief that they need to take the plunge. The follow-up is your opportunity to build further confidence, reinforce their belief, make them feel safe and supported, and educate them to the point that they are certain enough to take action.

If after the presentation they haven't yet committed to buying a set, during the fast-start training I will mention something like: "So obviously we need to get you on a set this week too. Where are you at with that?" in a no-pressure kind of way.

At the end of the day, *when* they sign up isn't important. But following the steps to achieve their dreams is!
There will be more details in the next section.

MILLION-DOLLAR TIP:
Master the testimonials. Role-play beforehand so that the testimonials are genuine, enthusiastic, to the point, and relevant to others.

Step Five: Following Up

"In network marketing the fortune is in the follow-up." —Eric Worre

Now I'm going to repeat this quotation because I really need you to understand that *the fortune is in the follow-up!* Despite this fact, next to nobody does it properly. Unfortunately, for a lot of people it seems as though the "do the bare minimum without getting fired" mentality that was learned in the workplace is difficult to change. When you bring those lazy habits into this business, many opportunities will be missed, especially when failing to follow up. So my suggestion is to become a master at it. When done properly, the follow-up is about education and support. You want to provide the prospect with enough information for him or her to be confident about getting started. All you are doing is allowing the natural relationship to progress, and it should happen organically. It should *not* involve nagging and pestering. Let's face it, who wants to hard-close and nag their friends or people they don't know? Not many of us.

In reality the entire process is just a follow-up. Everything is just a point of contact that builds the relationship and belief in the prospect. The invitation is the first point of contact; the presentation is the second; the follow-up phone call or meeting is the third; and the training, sign-up and future events are all just points of contact as well. But for this scenario, I'm going to talk about the time after which the. prospect has seen a presentation.

Here are some key points regarding following up:

-Focus on educating, not convincing.
Ultimately you don't want to have to use sales techniques to persuade people to get started. If you do, they are likely to drop off as quickly as they signed up because they never really made the decision for themselves. So it is much better to focus on education, this way we don't feel like a salesperson, and they don't feel like they've been sold to. Plus, their decision to join is their own, and they are more likely to stick to it.

- Eliminate FEAR. What have they got to lose?
The biggest reason people don't get started is because they are stuck in fear. Fear has been programmed into us since we were children, and we have been taught that everything is out to get us. But remember that nearly all fear is *false evidence appearing real* (FEAR), so saying something as simple as, "You have absolutely nothing to lose by trying it out," can be the difference between

a prospect getting started or not. I always find it fascinating when the same people that blow five hundred dollars on a boozy weekend treat a purchase that's half the cost like they are buying their first home. If I've built a strong enough relationship with the prospect, I will help to make the situation a little clearer for him or her by highlighting that he or she has everything to gain in this opportunity with absolutely no possibility of pain. The beauty of network marketing is that everyone can have a low-risk shot at achieving an incredible life and income, with the worst possible outcome being that they spend some money on products they would probably buy anyway—not to mention the education, self-development, and new network.

- Start on products.
If you are getting ums and ahs, sometimes the best thing to do is just get them on the products. A small amount of action is better than hesitation every time, and they may just fall in love with the products enough to get the belief and enthusiasm they need to start the business.

- *Always* offer new perspectives.
You've probably heard at some point before that 95 percent of human thoughts are negative. Well I think it's actually even higher than that. The fact is that you are going to hear a lot of negative perspectives, and some are so negative and so ludicrous that they don't even make sense. Now it's not your job to directly attack and dismantle those negative perspectives; your job is to educate and tactfully persuade. I was the master of the aggressive attack at the start, and trust me, it didn't work well. I discovered that you will be much better off accepting the perspective and simply saying, "Yep, you can look at it that way, or you could look at it like this—" and then offering a new perspective. I remember hesitating for weeks on end when I was starting out. I complained about everything to my sponsor, including the cost of shipping. Instead of attacking me directly and telling me that I should just get over it, he gave me this new

perspective to consider. He asked, "Would the likes of Donald Trump or Richard Branson be worried about a few dollars in shipping costs? Or would they see the opportunity at stake in launching a new country?" I think I was signed up within the minute. All I needed was to see the new and entrepreneurial perspective.

- Use the higher powers.
I never want to get caught in an opinion war with a prospect. Quite frankly I don't have the energy to waste. So to avoid this, I always refer to what the experts say and recommend—never to what I think! This is great because it also duplicates. It's very difficult for your prospect to argue with what the most successful people on the planet are all endorsing. So please use them to your advantage.

- Preparing the prospect for SNIOP (*susceptible to the negative influence of other people*).
You can improve the follow-up process by decreasing the influence of potential naysayers or negative people who are stuck in a fear-based sense of reality. People will create all kinds of drama. They will say things like, "No one ever succeeds at these things" or "You will lose all your money." (Which, I must add, is ludicrous, considering the low entry costs that the industry is known for.) People can be dramatic and downright nasty, so you don't want your prospects to be influenced by them. Just keep in mind that almost all negative people seem to be dead broke and have no right to be giving anyone advice.

- The stronger the relationship, the easier the follow-up.
There is nothing worse than trying to follow up with a contact and having him or her dodge your calls and ignore your text messages, and then have that awkward moment when you see that person in the street. The best way to get around this is to build such a bond that he or she will feel able to talk to you without being harassed. I always use the no-pressure approach here. So

if that individual isn't ready to get started following a presentation (I always ask), I'll take him or her through the "opt out" approach. It goes something like this: *Well that's cool. Look, I'll give you a call at this time tomorrow night, and you can let me know where you're at. Whether you want to jump on the big set or the small set or if you aren't ready tomorrow, that's fine, just let me know. We'll have a chat and go from there.*

-Goal-focused follow–up:
To master the follow-up process, we should be continually working to set up the next point of contact. If you're always locking down the next meeting, not only will your follow-up skills improve but your whole business will improve as well. So remember to never leave a meeting without setting up another point of contact: bring them to the next event, the next training, another party, a two on one—whatever! Just continue the points of exposures until they believe!

MILLION-DOLLAR TIP:
Sometimes the best follow-up is just building a friendship.

What does the whole process look like?
1) Invitation
2) House presentation
3) Follow-up with one-on-one meeting
4) Phone call to go through more details
5) Team event
6) Prospect signs up
7) He or she completes the fast-start training
8) He or she repeats steps one to seven

Now it really doesn't matter at which point the sign-up occurs. People are generally far too focused on getting the person signed up, whereas I am focused on getting them rich! When you have the latter mentality, the sign-up becomes less of a big deal and can happen organically. Now in saying this, do we always provide the opportunity to get started right away? Absolutely. If someone is ready to buy, I'm certainly not going to say, "'Hey now, don't jump into this right away. Go speak with your parents to check if they are okay with it.'"

Final story: If I could ____, would you ____?
You need to understand what the prospect truly wants. With this information you are able to present that individual with a proposition. My sponsor asked me what I wanted and proposed what I could do to get it. As a result, he got a strong confirmation of commitment from me. At the time, all I wanted to do was move to America because I thought it was the land of opportunity and a possible way for me to escape the system. So he asked me what I wanted and proceeded with, "If I could show you a way to work from a laptop so that you could live and travel wherever you wanted, would you do it?" My answer was, "*Yes.*" And from that point he had me. All I needed was to learn the system, and I was up and running.

Step Six: The System and Structure

"Your residual income is only as reliable as your system." —Dave Nelson

You can have all the hype and momentum in the world—launches, re-launches, and competitions, all of which I recommend—but you need a system that maintains your residual income, even when there are no special occasions and maybe the energy is a little lower. (Your system is your weekly organisation meeting, one-on-ones, parties and training sessions.) Often new teams will get off to a flying start and may even produce $20,000 in their first month, but if their system hasn't been built to support that type of production, it will quickly drop. It's an all too common occurrence to see this $20,000 diminish to next to nothing if there hasn't been a reliable system installed. I've seen people bring in thirty to forty reps personally but be left with no residual income because they never built a system. Every business on the planet utilizes and runs off a system: most notably, McDonald's, which has duplicated their fail-proof system twenty-nine thousand times across the globe! Network marketing systems are quite similar in that they are virtually fail-proof. However, people just don't follow them. With the low entry costs of network marketing, people just aren't as diligent as they would be if they had just spent $2 million on a McDonald's franchise. I think it's crazy because the results of a successful network marketing organization can outweigh any franchise.

Greater system *clarity* leads to *confidence,* which leads to *action,* which leads to *results.*

People need a simple plan for daily, weekly, monthly, and yearly action. After assessing my organization's results over the years and studying the top-producing network marketing company's systems, I believe that this is the best system outline:

Daily
- Meet two new people per day to add to your list.
- Get the interest-piquing tool to five people (via Facebook, e-mail, etc.).
- Check social media or team page for updates.
- 15 minutes of self-development

Weekly
- 1 x business organization meeting (2–15 people is ideal)
This weekly meeting is nonnegotiable. It should include a review of the previous week, recognition, and company updates as well as planning the week ahead.
- As many house presentations/parties as possible.
- As many one-on-ones as possible.
- 1 x webinar presentation.
- 1 x basic braining (online or in person).

Monthly
- 1 x city presentation at an actual venue (during the weeks we generally just do house parties).
- 1 x mega training event.

Yearly
- 4 x regional training events.
- National annual event.
- Global annual event.

* This is just a rough guide, of course
** You may also be thinking: "Wow, this is a lot of physical meetings for the New Era. Shouldn't it be going on online?" Well actually, I believe that while the rest of the world goes online, person-to-person business becomes more effective. People are losing human touch, and this is a great way to bring them together. Use the power of the Internet to improve communication and enhance the face-to-face system rather than replace it.
*** Communication: Creating a Facebook group or a group on WhatsApp is a great way to communicate with the entire organization and create a

forum-like community. It provides great social proof and daily updates to keep people focused on the mission.

**** This type of system is for serious builders only. Your average rep that just promotes a product and makes a little bit of money will drop off if you push this upon him or her.

PART THREE

Mind-set & Miscellaneous

IN PART TWO WE LOOKED AT THE BASIC NETWORK MARKETING skills and the system structures that are being used by the most successful companies today. But even with a perfect product, a perfect company, in a perfect economy, at the perfect time, with the perfect system, many people will still fail, for the same reason that they have failed in other areas in life—mind-set. But we are going to dig a little deeper. Rather than stopping at individual mind-set for success, we need to look at the collective mind-set, which I refer to as your team culture.

1. Building a Winning Culture

"The way a team plays as a whole determines its success. You may have the greatest bunch of individual stars in the world, but if they don't play together, the club won't be worth a dime." —Babe Ruth

What makes a winning culture?

What can we draw from winning sporting teams, like Manchester United, or from winning businesses like Apple?

What do they all have in common?

Start by visualizing your favorite (successful) sporting team. Some of the common recurring themes that I hear when doing this exercise are as follows:

> They have fun, smile, and enjoy each other's company.
> They care about each other and have each other's backs.
> They are disciplined and hold each other accountable to high standards and expectations.
> They expect to win and do so often.
> They have trust in one another, which is built with the integrity of the individuals.
> There is mutual respect among the group.
> The belief is massive!
> They unite a wide range of leadership qualities and styles.
> They have a diverse variety of strengths and work to each other's advantages.
> They stick to the plan, and the team always comes first.
> They are confident and sometimes verge on cocky.
> When they have to pull through, they do.
> They strive for greatness and don't accept mediocrity.
> They want to leave a legacy.
> They pride themselves on work ethic.
> They are mentally tough and resilient when faced with adversity.
> Drama and complaints are not tolerated.

The reason I highlight these key points is because they also apply to a successful network marketing team. As your organization grows you need to ask yourself the hard questions: Is the team disciplined? Do we pride ourselves on work ethic? Have I as a leader built confidence in the team? When we start asking these questions, we can identify where we can improve. Now I have seen network marketing companies take off quickly and make the fastest growing company lists. They flaunt their big checks in record time, but often (not always) these companies crumble as quickly as they arose. From an observer's point of view, I believe it is because they forgot about the most important factor of any network marketing company: the people. They forgot about creating culture, about the importance of strong bonds, and instead they were caught up in numbers and money. Now money is important—this is a business at the end of the day—but one doesn't work without the other. Financial results and culture are like bricks and mortar: for long-term residual income, you need both.

So the people in your organization always need to come first. Bonding and social events are a great way to ensure that you know your team's *why,* so make sure you get the group together and give everyone the opportunity to talk and express themselves. Identify what the team wants to stand for and what the team values are and study other successful teams and businesses from around the world to get ideas. I would use the points listed above as a checklist, almost as a written values list in a traditional company. Discuss what each point means to the team in a network marketing context.

In summary, culture is everything! If you can build a culture of people who have a united mission and the confidence and swagger of an elite sporting team with emotional trust and connection, you will have a force to be reckoned with in the business world.

2. The Power of Personal Development

"To double your income, triple your investment in self-development."
—Robin Sharma

Personal development is all about changing and developing the mind-set for success, as mentioned earlier. I believe that Harv Eker summed it up best when he said, "Your inner world creates your outer world." When most people start out in network marketing, they don't have much to show for their "outer world," which is why it's so important to work on their "inner world."

I think of the human brain as being similar to a computer hard drive. When we use a computer hard drive, we upload information with a USB or manually via a keyboard. The human hard drive is a little different because we don't have full control of what is being typed on the keyboard and uploaded. The "typing" is done from a young age by our parents, school teachers, society, TV programs, and people we surround ourselves with, and the information is stored in our subconscious mind. At this young age, our belief systems and habits are formed not by any choice of our own but by our surroundings. It isn't until we begin to work on self-development and become self-aware that we can start to take control of our own programming. Now there's a huge problem with this whole scenario. From a young age we are at great risk of being herded along with the masses to become broke, unhealthy, angry, and frustrated adults by our very own parents, who didn't know any better themselves. We are programmed with so many harmful, negative, and limiting thoughts that I would need to write a new book just to cover them all, but you get my point. So it's not until we raise our awareness and understand this that we gain control of our destiny. The only way to change the results that we are getting in life is to target the source of the problem—our mind.

So here is how I see it:
We have our subconscious thoughts that we don't even realize we have (from programming that's been engrained over time).
We have our conscious thoughts, which we are aware of but often have little control over, as we search for immediate gratification.

We take actions/make choices based on either of these two. These thoughts, actions and choices have a compounding effect over time that determines our results.

To regain control and get the results necessary for our dreams to become a reality, we need to do some reverse engineering. It's obvious that we need to change our actions to change our results, but it isn't quite as simple as that. We need to tap into a deeper level, but why? Well for example, everyone knows what decisions and actions need to be taken in order to be in great physical shape, but do we do it? Almost never. Our mind-set, subconscious thoughts, beliefs, and limitations stop us from taking the simple action steps to achieve the desired outcome. So to dig deeper, we need to adjust the subconscious and the conscious thoughts, and once we get these right, the necessary actions become easy, and the desired results follow.

So the question we must now answer is: How do we change the subconscious thoughts that have been imprinted over a lifetime? Well, obviously we can't undo the programming that has occurred up until the present time, but we can change the imprints that we are experiencing today. The law of association highlights the importance of carefully choosing the people that you surround yourself with because you will in some way be influenced by their negative programming, no matter how strong your defenses are. To escape the pitfall of negative mind viruses, we need to constantly feed our subconscious mind with positive self-talk that actually serves us. Leadership expert Robin Sharma talks about having breakfast with the people whose lives you want to be living. Now obviously we can't always be with them physically, but we can read their books, follow their social media pages, watch their YouTube clips, and begin to absorb their thoughts, beliefs, and mind-set into our own subconscious. Our programming has taken place over twenty plus years, so it can't be fixed overnight. But if the student is ready to make changes and is committed to consistency and persistence, then change can happen quickly. The pain I was in at the beginning of my network marketing career was the fuel I needed to take massive action and make drastic changes, and I'm convinced that the amount of reading and self-reflection I did was the key to making those changes. So get your team reading, learning, and enhancing their minds. It needs to be a vital part of the team culture.

So we're now aware of subconscious mind programming, but how do we change our conscious thoughts? First, any self-development that you invest in will help and have a positive effect, but the most important area to work on for the conscious mind is self-awareness. I believe that it's the key ingredient of all self-development because unless you raise awareness of what it is you are actually thinking and doing, you aren't able to stop and correct it.

Reflection and asking yourself questions are the best ways to raise your self-awareness:

What do I think about most during the day?
How was my energy during that meeting?
During today's conflicts did I embody the victim or the victor mind-set?
When taking action, did I fabricate excuses or act in spite of them?

Questions like these that encourage self-awareness and reflection will help to shape the conscious choices every day. As self-awareness becomes second nature and we become more advanced, we can begin to ask ourselves these questions at key times during the day, especially during decision-making processes. This is when you reach the highest level of leadership and begin to master the universe and your life.

Most people who come into network marketing aren't already millionaires and are carrying considerable baggage in the form of limiting beliefs and poor programming. As we can see by the above example, the only way to change and improve their results is to access and modify the core of the problem. This then leads to positive changes in thoughts and feelings to create the right actions.

Self-development should be a main focus at regional training events and even at basic trainings sessions. But the real magic happens when a culture of readers is developed. Because readers truly are leaders, and learners create top earners! So make sure that you edify great books, audio tapes, and speeches.

Here are my *"Fab Five"* books that have had the greatest effect on my life:

1. T. Harv Eker - *Secrets of the Millionaire Mind*
This was a life-changing book that helped me to understand the power of mind-set and the effect it has on life. It focuses on the mind-set required to make money and has practical ideas that are really easy to follow and implement into your life.

2. Dale Carnegie - *How to Win Friends and Influence People*
At the time I didn't really appreciate the effect this book would have on me. It is a blueprint of human beings and their drives and actions. If you want to understand people, you cannot miss this book!

3. Robin Sharma - *The Greatness Guide/The Leader Who Had No Title*
Robin Sharma's work is so well balanced. These books grounded me a lot and helped me to master not only my leadership but my whole life. If more people read his stuff, the world would be a much better and happier place.

4. Arnold Schwarzenegger - *Total Recall*
This book left me with the belief that anything is possible. I remember putting it down, taking a few minutes to reflect, and thinking to myself,

"Wow, by following Arnold's principles, it's possible for me to achieve *anything* that I want in this life." This book got me excited about life, raised my lid, and got me thinking on a much bigger scale. When I have fears or doubts (we all still do), Arnold always comes to mind, and I draw a lot of inspiration from the way he took action against all odds.

5. Darren Hardy - *The Compound Effect*
This book gave me an enormous amount of clarity on exactly what it takes to reach the highest levels of success. Darren Hardy is the publisher of *Success* magazine and has spent time with the most successful people in the world, analyzing exactly what they do. Implementing his methods on tracking my organization, mastering the basics, and focus was a game changer for my business. If you are serious about taking your business and life to a world-class level, you can't go past his online program *Insane Productivity*.

The Law of the Lid and Leadership

"The greatest discovery of our generation is that human beings can alter their lives by altering their attitudes of mind, as you think, so shall you be." —William James

The law of the lid suggests that your business can only grow to the extent that you do. This is a hard pill to swallow for some, especially the alpha male types with big egos (like myself when starting). But it's definitely true that your income reflects your mind-set. And while your income may have its ups and downs, it will always level back out in the long run to the level that you are playing at mentally. Every time that I hit a plateau in my business, I hit the books and developed myself further. Today I read more than ever before, and I'm always looking to learn new things, expand my consciousness, and expand my life so that I can expand my income.

Not only will you have to worry about your personal lid, but as your team grows you will need to deal with an organization lid too. This is why it's important to focus so hard on self-development and to instill it as a core aspect of the culture of the group. When multiple people develop together, it has a magical compounding effect that will see the members of your team feed off of one another's growth and lift each other up. It's a beautiful thing to watch!

So get reading. At the end of the day, the company has a vehicle that works; the industry works; the system is proven, but the rest is up to you. If you get your head right, you can make it happen.

Beware of the Leadership Traps

Focusing on "they" rather than "I":
I've been to a long list of self-development events over the past few years, and at every one I've found exactly the same people who were at the *sales strategy* training the week prior, the *mind-set training* the week before that, and the *unleash your potential* workshop the week before that! These people are enthusiastic, full of energy, and love every minute of these events; however, they don't really get any better at what they do. They don't apply any of the skills themselves because they are too busy trying to apply them to other people. They are trying to fix everyone—except themselves! These types often get a severe case of "know-it-all-ism." They have heard from all of the success speakers firsthand, and now feel as if they have a God-given calling to go out and fix other people! While helping others and applying the principles of these seminars to your team is a crucial part of network marketing, the point I'm trying to get across here is to not fall into the trap of focusing on everyone else's flaws instead of looking at yourself and facing your own demons or weaknesses.

Hiding behind learning:

The second trap that I see catching people out is the mistake of getting stuck in the "learning and developing" phase and not taking action. Now as important as developing your mind is, without applying the necessary actions on a daily basis, no amount of learning will build your business. I have seen people spend years "getting ready" and hiding behind their self-development as a way of feeling productive, but they just never take any action. I say this because although I'm the biggest advocate of self-development, like everything in life there's a fine line, and we need to balance action and learning. So if you can be wary of these traps, your self-development will be the best investment you ever make and worth every second of your time.

MILLION-DOLLAR TIP:

Don't wish for a million dollars. Instead work on creating the person who is worth a million dollars and who creates it as a by-product of your actions.

---

3. The Victim or Victor Mind-Set

"There is no such thing as a really rich victim." —T. Harv Eker

In every scenario that confronts us in life, we have the choice to respond as either a victim or a victor. A victim mind-set is one that sees the worst in everyone and everything, and a person affected by it usually believes that the world is out to get him or her.

As I mentioned earlier, some studies have suggested that 95 percent of human thoughts are negative, and by looking at today's society, I wouldn't doubt the validity of those studies. Negative thinking can be highly contagious, and when things aren't going our way nearly all of us fall into this trap. I know that even today I regularly find myself slipping back into my old habits, but fortunately because of the hours of self-development I've put in, I catch myself pretty quickly and turn my thoughts around. I believe that we're given a choice in every situation in life to either take the high road or the low road, and these choices have a compound effect over a prolonged period of time to ultimately shape the life we live.

Whatever you believe is true for you. So if you have a victim mind-set you will transfer these thoughts into reality and create scenarios in which you feel powerless. The same goes for the victor mind-set. You can create your own reality and the circumstances that you desire through your beliefs, thoughts and actions. You are not a victim of your circumstances, and the sooner you understand that you have created the results in every facet of your life, the sooner you can evolve and begin to shape-shift your own world.

Your victim/victor mind-set goes a lot deeper than your conscious thoughts, words, and actions. It ties back to your subconscious mind, where what you believe becomes true. Let me give you a scenario:

Let's use a situation that occurred in my organization. Imagine that person A goes into a meeting with an accountant that is making $90,000 per year. Person A's belief is that the accountant earns great money, that he is successful, and that he would probably never be interested in network marketing. But person A goes through with the meeting anyway because he was told to follow through with everyone on his list.

Person B considers the $90,000 per year that the accountant is earning and shakes his head. He thinks that it is awful money in this economy and feels that working inside an office for fifty hours every week sorting through paperwork and working on rich people's tax returns is a nightmare. He believes that the accountant will certainly understand the numbers and be excited by the idea of the compounding effect.

Who do you think will have a better result from meeting with the accountant? Person A creates an impartial response, and the accountant might try the products and have a think about the business. Person B gives the accountant an opportunity for a new lease on life and a feeling of excitement that he hasn't felt since his childhood. The accountant signs up and is excited to get to work right away.

Did the accountant have preconceived beliefs about persons A or B that altered the outcome of the meetings? Did person B have any advantages over person A? Of course not. So then what was the difference? They both presented the same opportunity using the same slide show, and the only difference was their mind-set.

The old saying "what you focus on expands" isn't just an old wives' tale. Modern science is now beginning to reveal the truth behind the idea that your thoughts are actually an energetic vibration that is sent out to the universe, similar to a radio transmitter. These thoughts have a magnetic effect, and Harv Eker says that when you complain about things, you automatically become a living, breathing crap magnet!

Have you ever noticed that when you are looking at buying say, a red Toyota, all of a sudden you see hundreds of red Toyotas everywhere you go? This is the law of attraction at work. What we focus on becomes a habit, and most people are not mindful of their thoughts. These are some really important questions to start asking ourselves: What do I think about often? Are my thoughts positive or negative? What effect do I have on others? Dr. John Demartini says that our quality of life is determined by the quality of the questions we ask. So start asking yourself the hard questions and being mindful of your thoughts. Once you realize what choices you are making, you can make changes for the positive, but when you aren't aware, you are like a blind person looking for answers.

Here are some examples of perceived problems. Does your brain focus on the negative or the positive outcome?

Your new distributor's order goes missing. Do you:
A) Play the victim: Send an angry message to the head office, complain about the company to your new rep and the team, and proceed to carry on like a headless chicken (you will be surprised by how many people will act like this).

or

B) Play the victor: Explain that these things are part of business and are out of the company's control. You proceed to explain that the company will work as quickly as possible to resolve the issue and provide a suitable solution. All the while you keep the new distributor's eyes on the prize and focusing on the big picture.

Scenario Two:

The customer doesn't reorder. Do you:
A) Play the victim, blaming everything and everyone except yourself. Here are a few common responses. "The company's products are too expensive." "All of my friends are broke." "No one in my

town is interested." "My contacts aren't as good as other people's." And so on and so forth.

or

B) Play the victor, taking responsibility realizing that you didn't establish the value, looking to improve for the next meeting, and continuing to focus on your vision.

Unfortunately, most of us have been programmed to play the victim.

Being negative is one of the easiest things in the world to do—followed by getting down on yourself, followed by being easily frustrated, and then followed by whining and complaining. Funny enough, mastering these character flaws is also the easiest way to stay broke! Most people today are wimps. They're too emotionally damaged to make the necessary positive changes in their life. Don't be that person—don't get stuck. The longer you spend continuing with your old habits, the harder it is to change them. The next time you catch yourself entertaining any kind of negative mind viruses, ask yourself: What would a positive person do? Or what would my hero say? And then switch your mind-set quickly! You created the negativity; it isn't real. So as the creator of it, only you can shift it. You have the power, so be sure to use it.

Utilize Newton's laws.
Newton stated that energy is never created or destroyed, only transferred from one form to another. Based on the information that we discussed earlier, we know that being negative or having a victim mind-set is a negative energy. Now if energy cannot be destroyed only transferred, we must not try to stop it. Rather, change it into a positive by raising your self-awareness and analyzing your responses to negative situations.

"If you knew how powerful your thoughts were, you would never think a negative thought." —*Peace Pilgrim*

4. Creating a Warrior Mind-Set

"The true warrior's greatest battle is the battle that lies within, the struggle to master the ego, to fight not for gain or glory, but to balance the scales of justice. Only when the mind is free of the concept of self can the hand strike swift and true." —*Bruce Lee*

In ancient times the most respected and revered warriors were physically strong and fit, but today, physical fitness alone won't get you far. As we've evolved over time, it's no longer necessary to master the art of fighting with sword and shield, but the same battles still remain, only in a different form. Today we must instead develop our mental and emotional strength and master the greatest weapon of all, the human mind.

There is no easy way for me to say this, but if you can't manage your emotions you won't make it here. Warren Buffett said it best: *"If you can't manage your emotions you will never manage money."* This is very true, and to add to it I would say that you will never manage a team either. You need to already have—or need to develop—a thick skin in this game, or any business for that matter. When working with hundreds of people, you will inevitably be forced to deal with their drama, their childish tantrums, and their immaturity. The list goes on. Believe me, you will see it all. If you aren't mentally strong and prepared, you will be taken on each of their emotional roller coasters, and they are not the fun kind that you find at the theme park! So if you don't learn to manage your emotions and understand "the way it is,'" this business could leave you needing therapy. It's become so common for people to over think the small things, take everything personally, and create problems that didn't even need to exist. So don't be too precious, don't take things to heart, don't read into things too much, and always be moving forward toward the end goal.

Be a rock.
In a world of emotionally unstable people, it's the stable ones that create an aura of power and wisdom about them. If you want to be highly respected and looked to as a powerful, influential person, then learn to control your emotions, *especially* when the shit hits the fan. The more people you work with, the more emotional instability you will see. There will be times when every inch of your being wants to unleash *your* thoughts on a particular ignorant person, but trust me, this doesn't serve anyone. You are far better off to stay calm and assess the situation from a new perspective. Network marketing gives you a great insight into what people are really like behind the public image they display on social media or at a dinner party on a Friday night. You are going to face thousands of people problems in your career that will range from seeing adults break down in front of you to receiving threats of being sued. I've seen people practically claim that the products saved their life one day and then turn around and ridicule the company the next. I've seen committed reps making good money disappear from the business and then all of a sudden return. You can't be shocked or upset by these things. Expecting to be able to build your business in a one-sided universe that's full of happy, sane, positive people is a delusion that will cause you much pain and suffering. We live in a perfectly balanced world: for every lover, there must be a hater, and for every positive, there must be a negative. So the idea that it's all going to be rainbows and butterflies is, in my opinion, the root cause of most network marketing pain and frustration. So please, please, please toughen up! As Sylvester Stallone said while playing Rocky in the latest sequel, "Let me tell you something you already know: the world ain't all sunshine and

rainbows. It's a mean and nasty place, and I don't care how tough you are, it will beat you to your knees and keep you there permanently if you let it. You, me, or nobody is gonna hit as hard as life. But it ain't about how hard you hit, it's about how hard you can get hit and keep moving forward. That's how winning is done!"

Now before I scare you all out of your minds here, you must understand the perfect balance of duality, positive and negative, good and evil in our universe. Once you understand the balance, the negative side will no longer affect you because you understand the reality of life, business, and "what is." I want to get you to that point as quickly as possible because once nothing affects you or gets you upset, you can enjoy every minute of this business and reach success at speed.

Detach from results.
Many Eastern philosophers believe that attachment is the root of all un-happiness, and I tend to agree. When you become attached to something, someone, or a particular result, you unwittingly attach your happiness to it as well. Overly attached people are generally very needy, which is an unattractive quality that will actually push the desired outcome further away. In this business, people can go all in and place their chips, hopes, and dreams on the success of a single person. People can put new reps on a pedestal with comments like, "This guy knows everyone!" And then they carry on as if the success of their network marketing career revolves around whether or not they get started in the business or not. It only takes a couple of experiences to realize that these scenarios never pan out the way we want them to. Detaching from the result in this business is the most powerful thing that you can do. It has a magical liberating power that can even have prospects chasing you. It's kind of like having a crush on someone at school: when you're too keen or are too attached, it almost

never ends well, and they usually make a run for it. It's the same in this business. There are hundreds of millions of people out there who are dead broke and who are looking for an opportunity like you have to offer, so there's absolutely no excuse for being needy or attached.

Rechannel your emotions.
To recap, controlling your emotions does in no way mean that you should cut off your emotions altogether. I'm simply saying that the ability to control and harness them in the right way can be a game changer for your business. The ability to effectively channel your emotions into your *why*, into your team's success and prosperity, into your internal drive, or when showing empathy is extremely beneficial!

5. Building Your Brand

"I'm not a businessman, I'm a Business Man! So let me handle my business damn." —Jay-Z

In the modern day and age, *you*, the individual, truly are a brand. It starts with how you dress, how you talk, and how you hold yourself, and if you're thinking that people shouldn't judge a book by its cover, well I have news for you—they do! We are judged by our Facebook account and by what comes up on a Google search; in today's world it all matters. Modern life has become part real/physical and part online, and if you position yourself well on both ends, you can make things much easier for yourself.

Remember that people don't buy into companies. No one wants to follow Virgin for example. But they do want to follow and engage with the company's charismatic founder, Richard Branson. In this business, people won't buy into your network marketing company; they will buy into you first and the company later. Look at reality TV shows. It's a booming television genre because people are interested in what others are doing all of the time, whether it be what we eat, what we think, or where we travel. If you can combine education with the ability for people to watch, follow, and fall in love with you, then wow, you have an incredible social media brand.

Your Facebook profile is no longer just a tool for connecting with your friends and family. It has become the billboard of your life. So if you want to be taken seriously in the world of business and attract people to your organization, then remove the victimhood posts and quit complaining about all of the things going wrong with your life. Also remove the photos of you being blind drunk in your underwear lying on the bathroom floor! But here is the key point. Work on making people jealous of your life in a tactful way. This is attraction marketing at its finest and can bring you a lot of easy business in the long term if done correctly.

Brands aren't built overnight, but you can certainly get started today. This means thinking about what kind of message you wish to send to others when they come across you. Once you're feeling clear enough about your image, go ahead and start a Facebook fan page and add value, document parts of your life, and start building.

Here are three key elements that you should consider when building your brand: First, know where you want to end up, know what you want to become, and know what you are going to add to the world. For example, where do you want to end up? Do you want to end up being one of the greatest network marketers of all time? Do you want to be the next Jim Rohn? Or do you just want to build an amazing platform that allows you and hundreds of your friends to share financial freedom and success?

What value will you add to the world? Are you going to be the best mentor or write a book? Will you be a great public speaker? What problems will you fix? Whatever it is that that you choose to do, make sure that the *why* is crystal clear in order to make it easier to start building the person you want to be (your brand). If you really want to get in depth with this stuff, *Crush It* is a great book by Gary Vaynerchuk in which he discusses the importance of building your brand and even monetizing it.

MILLION-DOLLAR TIP:

Think about how others see you. Ultimately the market's perception of you is your brand. Do they know what you are about? What your intention is? What you can do for them? If not, start creating a plan to change this!

---

6. Adapting Like a Chameleon

"Intelligence is the ability to adapt to change." —Stephen Hawking

People do business with people they like, love, trust, and respect. But as we know, mixing different personality types creates challenges, personality clashes, and differences of opinion. So having intuition and the tact to build strong relationships is a key factor in this business. If people don't like you, they simply won't end up working with you long term. People join tribes or groups of people that are just like them; it's happened since the beginning of time. But the problem is that most people just aren't like you! However, we do all experience the same universal problems, and it's not difficult to find a common interest with just about anyone. So this is where you have to be understanding, compassionate, and able to adjust to connect with people from all walks of life. The more people you can connect with, the larger the team you can lead, and I also believe that this greater connection will enhance your experience of life.

Being a chameleon is very similar to Bruce Lee's philosophy: "Be water, my friend." When water is in a tea cup, it becomes the tea cup, and when in a glass, it becomes the glass. You really need to be able to put yourself in other people's shoes and connect, no matter how different they may be to you. We are all different in so many ways, but we are also the same in so many ways too. If you really want to be a next-level person on the planet and if your goal is to influence as many people as possible, then you need to be an expert at seeing the world from other people's perspectives. You need to dig deep and understand their feelings, frustrations, and fears.

Intuition

There are going to be times in your network marketing career when you have to play the *good cop,* and there will be times when you will have to come down on people and play the *bad cop.* There will be some people whom you will go easy on and others whom you can push and apply pressure to in order to get the best out of them. This is where you need to use your intuition. If you don't use your intuition already, it will come quite quickly if you pay attention because every action has a reaction, and you will soon notice patterns (reactions) with your approaches to certain people. If one approach isn't working, try another! This isn't something we're taught at school and that is advanced stuff if you're new to the industry, but it is highly important. We need to become aware of our intuition by noticing what effect our actions have on others. After all, we live in a world of cause and effect. The same goes for meetings. Some people can be pushed hard, while others will be highly offended. Some will respond well to attacking questioning, and others won't. This is all stuff that takes time and practice to master. But you will get better at it.

MILLION-DOLLAR TIP:

Raise awareness of how you speak to people and how you make them feel. Raise awareness of the reaction to your actions or the effect of the cause rather than just going about your business brazenly.

"If you don't understand, you suffer."

These were the wise words told to me by my mentor and company founder during our first meeting. I didn't fully understand it at the time, but I knew that down the track I would. To manage a large team you must have a certain level of understanding of people. You need to have compassion, and instead of being frustrated at what certain team members might be doing, try to understand *why* they are doing it. If you don't bring yourself to understand the people in your team, you will be the one to suffer from continual conflict and frustration. So be kind and compassionate—it's *not* a sign of weakness.

Chameleon leadership:

I believe that every great leader has multiple sides to his or her character, and that there's a time and a place for all of them. There are times to be fun and playful, serious and hyperfocused, humble and appreciative, and even at times vulnerable, and there are certainly scenarios where it's necessary to be firm, direct, and even sometimes critical. Now the secret here is to know your audience. I am certainly not going to go *Boiler Room*-style on a new group of fragile reps. But if business is slow with my leaders that have truly decided and are able to handle it, there will be times when coming down on people with some bittersweet truth is essential.

Another trait of the chameleon leader is to know how some individuals and teams within the organization respond to pressure and competitions. There are always the people who you can and can't push, who run for competitions, and who crumble at the thought of one! And of course there are the people who will take praise and edification modestly in their stride and those whose ego will get the better of them. All of these factors can be judged when we start to raise awareness of the actions and begin looking at the reactions. You will start to see patterns.

Recognition:
So far in this chapter we have overviewed how different we all are, but when it comes to recognition and appreciation, it is something that all of us crave—yes even you, and certainly me! It's ingrained in our DNA, and some people say that "babies will cry for it, but adults will just about die for it." So you need to dedicate a certain percentage of every event, every meeting, and every training session to recognizing and showing appreciation for those who deserve it. Now don't just praise results; it's important to praise effort too. Everyone wants to feel appreciated, heard and loved. We may as well live with an "I need love" sticker permanently stuck to our foreheads! But while we're on the topic, don't stop here. Listening is such an underutilized thing these days. One of the greatest gifts that you can give to someone is both of your ears and your undivided attention. Giving the time of day to hear someone's opinion and ideas is extremely rare and highly appreciated. If you want a great energy and vibe in your team, then make sure that your recognition is through the roof! Prizes, cars, and cash bonuses are great for this, and they also create drive for the people coming up through the ranks.

7. Managing Your Time

"There is nothing so useless as doing efficiently that which should not be done at all." —Peter Drucker

These days it is almost impossible to get the most simple of tasks completed without distractions from social media and technology. For example, when I began to write this book, I would literally only be able to write three lines before my phone would go off, my Facebook would beep with the sound of new instant messages, or I would get a call on Skype! So I had to turn off all of my devices and set a timer for a thirty-minute block in which I could dedicate 100 percent of my attention to the task at hand. The same applies in network marketing, and I swear that some people get more invitations done in thirty minutes of concentrated effort than others do in an entire month. Today, in a fast-paced world, if you want to be an elite performer, you need to be very efficient with your time. There's no time for overthinking, no time for procrastinating—only time for doing!

The 80/20 rule suggests that you spend 80 percent of your time with your top 20 percent and only 20 percent of your time with your bottom 80 percent. Over the last one hundred years of business, it has been discovered that the top 20 percent will always produce 80 percent of the results (or thereabouts) in almost every area of life. A big time trap that many network marketers should be wary of is the needy reps. Whether it's because they didn't receive enough attention at home or at school, they will take advantage of your supportive nature and suck your energy. This is where the 80/20 rule becomes very effective. As the great philosopher Jim Rohn says, you need to give to those who deserve, not those who need.

Another common time management problem is working out how much time to spend on helping the team as opposed to frontlining and bringing in new business yourself. I tend to like the 80/20 rule for this also, but in this circumstance it can go both ways. By this I mean that if you are a brand-new rep, 80 percent of your time should be spent on bringing in new business, and 20 percent of your time should be spent on working with your down-lines. Over time, and as the team grows in size, 80 percent of your time should be spent on working with the team, and only

20 percent should be spent on bringing in new business. I believe that the biggest mistake people can make is to very quickly spend 100 percent of their time on their team and 0 percent on their own production. Remember the saying: monkey see, monkey do? If you're not bringing in new business, often the team won't either.

Part-time vs. full-time:
I still believe that this business is best started part time, not full time. When we have too much time on our hands and not a big enough team to fill in the hours, we become lazy, can overthink, and seem to get stuck. This business can boom on as little as ten hours per week. I know that many of you reading this are thinking, "But I don't have ten hours a week!" I bet those same people spend at least twenty hours a week on Facebook, Twitter, and Instagram. We can all make time if we just become a little more organized and efficient.

Order of priorities:
Tony Robbins, the world-renowned success coach to some of the most talented and successful people on the planet has an extensive time management program that is said to be used by all of his billionaire clients. The most important element of the program is to discover which activities lead to the outcomes that you want. Therefore, whichever activities produce the best outcomes need to be prioritiszd. So in network marketing, you can never replace inviting prospects, presenting, and following up. These are obviously the first things that should be placed into your schedule. Self-development, as well as reading, is important, but it doesn't produce direct outcomes, so these along with the weekly team meeting must be scheduled later. Don't just stop with your network marketing business; structure your whole life in this way and start living in line with your highest values and the things that serve you and your greatest vision.

Learn to say no.

I've done a lot of reading on the late Steve Jobs and the great Warren Buffet—two of the most successful people in history, and they both make time to mention the power of saying *no. Yes men* are continually caught up in meaningless tasks because they want to please everyone else over themselves. They hate confrontation, and although they may avoid short-term pain by acting this way, it creates long-term pain in their lives. Trust me: half of the people that you are worried about pissing off don't feel the same way toward you. They won't cry when you die, and they probably won't add any real value to your life. So it's not selfish to put yourself first, it's noble!

Productive vs. busy:

This is the great entrepreneurial challenge. We don't have a boss barking orders at us, and we aren't sat down each morning with a to-do-list that must be finished before we go home. But when we become self-employed, all of a sudden it's easy to confuse being busy for being productive. So my advice is to create a self-motivated to-do list, with your "result-focused activities" at the top rather than just "busy work."

Meeting times:

I have noticed that successful businesspeople always keep their meetings short and sharp and conduct them with a very clear purpose. Only block out an hour for meetings. Value and respect your own time, and other people will begin to respect it too. Remember that the goal of a meeting isn't for it to be extensive; it's to set up the next one.

8. Success Characteristics

"The most successful people I've worked with, like the Rolling Stones—people of a different, kind of legendary caliber—have such great, warm energy." —Christina Aguilera

Here is my favorite exercise for tapping into that energy for success: Imagine that the most successful person you know of (I thought of Richard Branson) is stepping out of a limousine to walk down a red carpet and into a luxury resort. What expression is on his or her face? How does he or she interact with others? What do you notice about that person?

I think that molding is one of the most powerful ways to own the traits of the most successful people on the planet. You can mold not only their thoughts, beliefs, and words but even their body language as well. All body language sends triggers throughout your system that your entire body responds to. So if you want to obtain the same responses as the people you admire, molding even the smallest of things like posture and hand movements can make a big difference in the way you speak and think.

One of my favorite authors, Dr John Demartini, suggests picking out a number of people that you admire and then listing the characteristics that you admire the most about them. As a result of his research, Demartini has come to believe that we vibe with the traits of others that we actually already possess within ourselves. So if you list three people and their three characteristics, you will have nine desirable characteristics to make your own (some characteristics may overlap, so there may be less). According to Demartini, this is an indication of who you truly are, and it's a fantastic guide for who you should build yourself to become. It's a fascinating exercise. I do it every morning, and it has really shaped who I am today.

Test it out for yourself. Stop reading and take a couple of minutes to think of three people that you admire:

Person One:

Trait One:

Trait Two:

Trait Three:

Person Two:

Trait One:

Trait Two:

Trait Three:

Person Three:

Trait One:

Trait Two:

Trait Three:

Here is a list of characteristics that many successful people have adopted:

Humor and smiles;
If you can exhibit a smile and a sense of humor at your presentations and meetings, it screams success to people's subconscious minds. When the nerves set in, it's easy to lock up and become far too serious, which can be really unattractive to somebody in the audience. This is why smiling and adding the odd joke can be such a powerful tool. If you are relaxed and having fun, people will be far more likely to buy into you and what you're doing. So smile, laugh, and have fun, without trying to be the class clown. It's still your job to execute the plan, lock down the follow-up meeting, ask the tough questions when necessary, and not be walked over.

Tip: When you're nervous about meeting with a prospect who intimidates you, be respectful, but never put them on a pedestal. Smile more, laugh more, and try having a good time, which will make you seem much more relaxed, comfortable, and confident.

Controlled emotions:
As mentioned earlier, very few people today—or throughout history, for that matter—are able to control and contain their emotions. If you can master your emotions, you instantly receive an aura of power, control, and success. Now I am certainly not saying to be emotionless or cold, but I am saying learn to control it and don't react immediately to situations. Understand that the first minute after any scenario is the worst time to react. This is when you are running on emotions, not logic, so whenever conflict occurs, sit back, don't react, take the noble road, and use your mind.

Be a good person:
I know that society has us programmed to believe that rich and successful people are greedy and evil, but from my experience, this simply isn't true. I

have found that wealthy people have a genuine concern for people. They want others to do well, and they want to help others become successful where they can. So simply being a good person is one of the most admirable things you can do. People will notice, and most importantly the universe notices too!

Stay hungry:
"Your deepest expectations ultimately create your results." Successful people have a huge expectation on what they will achieve in this lifetime. There is nothing sexier than someone who is driven, has big dreams, and relentlessly chases them!

Certainty:
Successful people ooze certainty. Tony Robbins said it perfectly: "He who is most certain influences the other person every time." If your goals and dreams are clear, your plan has been mapped out, and you have practiced your ability to articulate and share your message, you too can release that certainty. In an uncertain world, people are looking for the certain, strong leaders to guide them.

"For me life is continuously being hungry. The meaning of life is not simply to exist, to survive, but to move ahead, to go up, to achieve, to conquer."
—*Arnold Schwarzenegger*

9. Improving Retention

"I think the acquisition of consumers might be on the verge of being mapped. The battlefield is going to be retention and lifetime value."
—*Gary Vaynerchuk*

The most frequently asked question that I have had during my career is: "How do we make people take action and become inspired?" It's the trillion-dollar question for not only this industry but for life in general, and unfortunately there is no silver-bullet answer. I can't just say "do this" and get everyone to stick to it. The reality is that not everyone can be saved, and not everyone will reach their full potential in this lifetime. The answers lie in the basics, which is true for everything in life.

But in saying this, and as much as I understand it, I have always taken it upon myself to do my bit and fulfill my half of destiny, which I choose to do for every aspect of life. I've come to learn that the most successful people on the planet aren't busy looking for short cuts; they are busy mastering the basics.

Let's now review some of the basics to see how they are fundamental in improving retention:

- Why
I've said it before, and I will say it again, because it is so important: The strength of your business always boils down to the strength of the *why*. If you do a thorough job of accurately establishing your new rep's values, goals, and underlying reasons for starting the business and then explain how the network marketing business model can make those ambitions a reality, your retention will improve. People live for their highest values, so you can always get more commitment when you nail this properly. As soon as someone identifies his or her goals and believes that he or she can achieve them with this vehicle, magic happens! But barely anybody does a sufficient job of this.

- Daily contact
The more contact you have with your team members, the less likely they are to drop off. It's your job to provide an alternative perspective when they get negative and brush them off after their first naysayer experience.

Over time their belief in themselves becomes stronger, and it will have been worth the time.

- Drip-feed ABC

In the sales world, ABC is known as *always be closing*. In the network marketing world, closing doesn't stop once the prospect gets started; in fact, it never stops. You need to keep selling your team on the company, the industry, and on themselves. People fall into a state of negativity so easily and lose belief quickly, so you need to continue to build and project confidence throughout the team. I've become a master at creating hype. I remember when Avon signed Megan Fox and Herbalife signed Christiano Ronaldo. I was selling the story extremely hard to the team! You may be thinking, "Why on earth would you promote another company?" Well, it's all about how we set up the message. I would say things along the lines of, "Can you see where this industry is heading?" and "This is going mainstream and will be bigger than franchising; the best of the best are aligned with what we do!"

Learn to turn everything into a positive and to create confidence, belief, and hype. CNS: *closing never stops.*

- System

A weekly system is the only way to keep people committed all year round. Without one, people go missing and inevitably get caught up in drama and distractions that hurt their business. Just like I said earlier, if you don't have a system, you don't have true residual income.

- Leadership and personal development

Getting the team into a habit of daily personal development as soon as possible will elevate their thinking patterns and belief systems to a point where they are no longer affected by the thought of failure or by the negativity of others.

- You

The more you take charge, lead by example, and get results, the more inspiration you provide for your team. Sometimes you can't save everyone, but you *can* always be the best that you can be.

"*No man can properly command an army from the rear. He must be at the front…at the very head of the army. He must be seen there, and the effect of his mind and personal energy must be felt by every officer and man present with it.*" —*General William T. Sherman*

- Appreciation and recognition

The only things that we humans care about more than sex and money are recognition and appreciation. You *must* dedicate some time each week to recognize and appreciate people within the team. This is probably the most effective way to keep retention high, considering that genuine appreciation is so rare these days.

-Value

Einstein put it best when he said, "Try not to become a man of success, but rather try to become a man of value." This quotation literally changed the game for me. It was something I used as my screen saver and continued to refer back to whenever I was stuck—to get my focus in the right direction again. So add value to your team. Make sure that you give them a call for support (this is value), send them a great article (this is value), and send them a success story that builds their belief (this is all value). All you need to focus on is adding enough value to the team, and if you do it on a large enough scale, you uncover the secret to great riches. Generally your wealth will be connected directly to the amount of people you add value to. Why is Branson so rich? Why is Bill Gates so rich? Well, they add value to billions of people across the globe with services that improve people's lives.

10. Inspiring Action with a Locker-Room Speech

"There is no passion to be found playing small—in settling for a life that is less than the one you are capable of living." —Nelson Mandela

I've always drawn great inspiration from movies. I believe they are laden with truths and full of life lessons, and I think they are a great hobby to have within reason. There is nothing more inspirational than the call-to-action speech by William Wallace in *Brave Heart* when he rallies his troops to fight for their freedom or the famous Al Pacino halftime speech in *Any Given Sunday* when the team has the odds stacked against them.

My favorite method for generating massive action is definitely "the locker-room speech." It's not hard to see that we are emotional beings because we're certainly not logical ones! Emotion drives extreme action; a man on a mission can move mountains. To have the locker-room speech with someone, you require a sense of connection, and he or she needs to know that you care and have his or her best interest at heart. It is similar to sharing your *why*, except that during the locker room speech you may be a little more off-the-cuff. You may be a little raw, a little more honest, a little less politically correct; you may drop the odd F-bomb if the time and place is right; you may dig a little deeper into the pain, be a little more philosophical, and hell, you may even be a little inspirational!

So I'm dead serious when I say go home and watch your favorite movie speech, practice your own, own it, and go share it with people. It will not only be great for getting people started, it will be a great way of reigniting action. I signed up a lot of the world's top fitness professionals and models when I got started. I had been in that industry and had done quite well, so I sat them down and had the talk. I will leave out my colorful language, but it went along the lines of this:

> - We are the top fitness personnel in the country and are highly respected.
> - We are sharp, smart, good looking, young—we tick all the boxes.
> - Yet we are dead broke and slaving away in the rat race.
> - This s*** has to stop! We need to put an end to this now!
> - We can use this vehicle to create a movement of young, inspirational entrepreneurs.
> - The industry has never seen anything like this—nor has the world. We can leave a legacy.
> - Let's bind together, have a no-risk crack at having it all: the health, the wealth, the life, the success, the camaraderie.
> - So here is how this is going to go down (sell the plan).

That's just an example, but you can get a good idea of how to balance the focus on the pain and gain, drawing the line in the sand and selling a plan with certainty. You can tailor it for just about any situation or any group of people. Try it out for yourself and be sure to let me know how it goes.

11. Building Your Net Worth through Your Network

"Your network will determine your net worth." —Anonymous

While this quotation holds true in the game of life, it is even more applicable to the game of network marketing. Meeting and connecting with new people is one of the key skills of a professional in this industry. The secret to building your network is developing relationships with people *without* the intention of recruiting them into your organization. The secret to meeting a lot of people is extremely simple: smile, be outgoing, and ask people about their day with enthusiasm, and you will be a net-working magnet. People want to be around happy, fun, energetic people, so in network marketing I recommend bringing your energy to the game of life every day. Prepare each morning like an athlete would for a big game: get yourself into a peak state, think positive and happy thoughts, come from a place of love and understanding, and meet people with the mind-set that every person offers a lesson worth learning.

I recommend moving around a lot to broaden your network. Don't stick to the same hairdresser, for example, if the staff are a low energy bunch with little value to offer and unsuited for your business. Ensure that people remember you when you leave because you will find that you create an element of intrigue about you, and intrigue is the most attractive quality of a network marketer. You want people thinking to themselves, "What does this guy do? He sure smiles a lot, so I am certain he is a big success." If you can do this successfully, people begin to ask you what you do, and then *let them do the pitching for you!*

Building a strong network comes with numerous advantages. You will find yourself receiving discounts everywhere you go; you will get tip offs on good deals and "insider information," and when people know what you do, you will receive referrals! Most importantly though, you and the people you meet will have a better day, thanks to a simple smile and a little friendly conversation.

The key to enhancing your charm and getting people to like you is to show some genuine interest in their favorite topic of all: *themselves.* If you ask lots and lots of questions and then actually listen to their answers, people will be eating out of your hand and speaking well of you in no time! Most people today don't have anyone who truly listens to them at all, let alone someone who asks them questions. Most people are just waiting for their turn to talk, so you can stand out from the crowd with an unfair advantage if you can master this skill. You won't only have a big network, you will have a network that loves you!

12. The Law of Process

"Most people can't handle boredom. That means they can't stay on one thing until they get good at it. And they wonder why they're unhappy."
—*50 Cent*

Let me be straight with you: network marketing is harder than we expect it to be, and we all have the same disbelief as to why people don't get started and take a no-risk shot at their dreams when they have nothing else going for them. We get very frustrated in this industry as we struggle to articulate what we have; we get frustrated at our own team members who can't always help themselves; and often when we experience too much frustration, it becomes too stressful for us, and we quit.

The good news is that it gets easier.
The Law of Process takes effect.
We become wiser.
We develop emotional strength.
We get better.

Why do we have to wait? Why do we have to go through the law of process to reach success? Well, before I answer that question, I'm not saying that you have to build the business slowly. I was able to build a sizable income of more than double the average wage by the back end of my first year. However, once the law of process began to take effect, I started making a lot of money, and wealth became far easier for me to acquire. Instead of always approaching people, they began to approach me, and the work I put in when I followed up three to eight times started to pay off. Some of my best reps got started twelve to twenty-four months after I first pitched to them. It just wasn't their time; they weren't ready, and had I quit too soon (like most people would have), I would have missed out on all of the growth that these reps have produced!

As we have already discussed in previous chapters, your mind has been programmed throughout your entire life, so it can't be changed overnight. Yet that mind-set change is the only thing that can change your outcome! So it is going to take two to four years for you to learn and develop a millionaire mind and reap the results of that thinking. Everybody is on their own journey. Some will adapt and change fast; others will take some more time.

The test of time creates proof, and once you have done something for a long enough period of time you gain credibility—that's how the human brain works! There are so many gimmicks these days, and so many people trying out new things that they end up quitting within weeks. We all got sucked into buying exercise equipment like the *Ab Swing Pro* that never left our garage, and I'm betting that we probably never got those shredded abs we hoped for either. So naturally, people are skeptical of anything new, but once their pain is great enough and they know that you are still doing the business, the game changes.

Most people don't stick this game out long enough for their contacts to reach a point of pain and give the business a go. I used to be in the personal training industry, and I knew what kind of pain came with that industry just one to two years after starting. Any new career is generally fun at the start, but then the pain will kick in soon after, and it's this pain period when most people decide to make some changes. You know how it goes: we wait until we have a heart attack and nearly die before we start eating a healthier diet. The same goes for this business. We wait for the pain of our career and associated poverty to set in before giving network marketing a go. But what you as a rep must realize is that if you quit before your prospect reaches that crucial point, he or she is likely to go somewhere else and try a different network marketing company.

In addition to the law of process, I'm a big believer in there being a higher force—universal laws, God, whatever it is that resonates with you. I believe that this higher power just knows and rewards those who pay their dues. In our society, most people can't stick to anything long enough to be successful. They are scattered in every direction by distractions; their emotions are on a roller coaster ride, and they can't focus on the task at hand for a long enough period to become a master at what they do. Network marketing only requires a few very basic skills, but people don't stick to the basics, and they instead try to reinvent the wheel because their own boredom steers them away from the method that works. So it's all about consistency. My advice is to not only stick out the journey but stay consistent with your emotions and actions—because you will be rewarded!

The Compound Effect in Network Marketing

Now I want to show you the most conservative worst-case scenario that will demonstrate the power of this vehicle and how the law of process and the compound effect come into play.

So it starts with just you, a new rep with a busy schedule and very little time to put into the business. All that you can commit to is getting five guests to see a presentation each week. Five per week is twenty guests per month. Now let's imagine that your closing and follow-up skills are terrible, and you only get about one out of ten. This plan brings you in two new reps per month.

So if you are signing up only two new reps per month, you would have a total of twenty-four reps by year's end. Let's imagine that your retention rate is horrible, and five out of six drop off. Using that calculation, you would have a tiny team of only four reps by the end of year one. Not a lot of reward for your effort, right?

During year two, let's imagine that all four reps follow the same principle of growing by two reps per month. You would now have ninety-six reps by year's end, but with the retention rate of five out of six, only sixteen reps would still be running the business.

During the third year, all sixteen reps follow the same principle of just two new reps per month. You would have 384 reps by year's end, and taking into account the retention rate, you would have a medium-sized team of sixty-four active reps by the end of year three.

Through year four, all sixty-four reps stick to the two-per-month principle. By year's end you now have 1,536 reps, with only 256 being active due to the low retention rate. Your organization is now a little more impressive, but it's still not enough to retire on.

In year five, all 256 reps follow the same principle, and by year's end you now have 6,144 reps, with 1,024 reps being active.

Your team of 1,024 reps follow the same principle of two per month through year six, and your organization becomes 24,576 reps strong, with a whopping 4,096 being active given the retention rate.

During year seven, all 4,096 reps follow the same principle of two sign-ups per month, reaching a total of 98,304 by year's end, which whittles down to an incredible 16,384 active reps by the end of year seven given the retention rate of five out of six people dropping off. So what kind of money are we making now?

Well, again, let's be very conservative and say that all of the 16,384 reps only have a consumer base of two hundred dollars' worth of orders per month, which totals $3,276,800 in production. Most compensation plans pay approximately five percent on revenue, so for argument's sake, that would be a profit of $163,840 per month or more than $1.9 million per year. Not bad!

Now let's see what we are looking at when we use some slightly more realistic numbers. Let's imagine that the 16,384 reps had only four to five customers and instead of two hundred dollars' worth of orders per month, we used a conservative number of six hundred dollars. Now your annual income is closer to the $6 million mark.

The problem with this calculation is that most people never get to see these results because they quit in month three, six, twelve, or even thirty-six, when they aren't being well compensated for the work they are putting in. I didn't make a cent in my first three months, but looking back now, it's clear that the lessons I learned during that period have since earned me a fortune. As far as I was concerned, I was making money; I just hadn't been paid out yet. Most people quit before the payout. My advice is this: you are going to be working for the next seven years anyway, and hey, if you're Gen Y like me, you will probably be working the next fifty! So why not put five to ten hours a week into something that can set you up for life. Because let's be honest, at your job the only thing you will probably get after seven years of blood, sweat, and tears is a fancy pen and a thank-you card to go with your redundancy letter.

13. The Law of Sacrifice

"Human progress is neither automatic nor inevitable...Every step toward the goal of justice requires sacrifice, suffering, and struggle; the tireless exertions and passionate concern of dedicated individuals." —*Martin Luther King, Jr.*

When presented with the network marketing opportunity, people often ask, "So what's the catch? It sounds too good to be true!" Well, the catch is that it takes work, time, and sacrifice. It may mean missing your favorite TV show; it may mean missing drinking sessions; it may mean you see your partner a couple of times less a week; it may be any number of things. But there's one thing that I am sure of. Whatever you sacrifice will be more than made up for in the future. You need to give up the things that you *kind of* want to obtain the things that you *really* want. This is the law of sacrifice, and it has been known and understood since the beginning of time.

There is an unexplainable universal power that becomes evident when you begin to give things up, bend your will, and have discipline. When you have the discipline to control your urges, the universe notices and begins to bend things in your favor. A classic example of the power of sacrifice lies in our small decisions. As a society, we are searching for immediate gratification: we want instant pleasure and lots of it (at any cost).

Let's look at something as simple as dieting. When we are out for dinner and the dessert menu comes around, more often than not we go for the pleasurable option, even though we know that the long-term pain is unwanted body fat and diabetes. Our brains seem to block out the future result. It happens in this business too: we would rather enjoy the immediate pleasure of sitting on the couch and watching our favorite TV show than going to a company presentation or meeting. We know that the long-term pain from our lack of action is that our business won't grow; we will stay broke; we will stay stuck and miserable, but again, the human brain seems to ignore these long-term results and instead has an obsession and burning desire for instant gain. As the great Jim Rohn says, "You will either suffer the pain of discipline or the pain of regret." I can tell you now that the pain of discipline is the only thing that will bring you long-term pleasure. We need to raise our self-awareness of these small but influential decisions that we make in order to reverse the situation. We almost need to hypnotize ourselves in order to stay focussed on the long-term result in every decision we make. I believe that the only way to do this is to truly know what our goals in life are. This is the reason why visualization and *why* building is so important. Once we have a clear vision of who we want to be and why we want to be it, we can begin attaching our highest values and goals to every choice we make. We need to become obsessed with our goals and dreams so that we think about them all of the time, and they are subconsciously taken into account when making small decisions that ultimately have a large effect on our future. Self-awareness is everything, and it is strongly linked with the law of sacrifice.

What did I sacrifice? Well I will be very honest with you. I worked my butt off when I started out, and sleep was the first thing that I missed a lot of. I wouldn't be home until after midnight—most nights of the week. I burned the candle at both ends and had my body shut down on me several times throughout the year for a twenty-four- to forty-eight-hour period, pleading with me to slow down. But I couldn't slow down. I could see the success, I could see my life and dreams unfolding, and I was willing to give up a few hours of sleep for that! Now, does everyone have to do this? Absolutely not. But remember, I got my results much faster than 99 percent of network marketing success stories. But I did work for it! I was dead broke during my first months, and I remember at Christmas time, spending the last two hundred dollars in my account on a ticket to Sydney to expand. I stayed in a filthy motel and split the cost with a buddy I was building with. I didn't buy the family any Christmas gifts that year, but these days I can afford to fly them up to my beachside condo to see me at any random month of the year. Do you think they are upset about the jocks and socks they missed out on? Of course not. I missed a lot of gym time too, which was my favorite thing to do at the time. This saw me lose most of the muscle mass I had worked so hard for over the years. I went six months without doing more than a few push-up and sit-up sessions on the floor, but before you start feeling too sorry for me, today I often manage to have two sessions a day if that's what I feel like doing.

14. Dismantling Rejection

"I've come to believe that all my past failure and frustrations were actually laying the foundation for the understandings that have created the new level of living I now enjoy." —Tony Robbins

From my experience in the industry, I have come to understand that there is no such thing as rejection. You will never be told, "No," but you will be told, "Not yet." I have seen the most negative and the most cynical of people turn around and join what they once criticized vehemently. Yet when most people come into the profession and someone doesn't bite the very first time that they speak to him or her, they cross that person off their list and complain to their up-line: "No one is interested, wah, wah, wah."

Even in traditional sales it's said that 80 percent of sales take place between the third and eighth point of contact or exposure to the product/opportunity. Although many of us can get people started on the first one or two, the reality is that these numbers don't lie. Understand that not everyone is ready to buy products or get started in the business this week; the reality is that most people won't make a change until they are in pain. Again, when do most people go on a health kick? When their doctor tells them that if they don't lose weight they will die! It's the same with our opportunity, but once you have planted the seed, the next time they are at their dead-end job or the next time their boss treats them like dirt, you spring to mind, and the law of process comes into play.

When someone reacts negatively to you, don't take it personally. You never know what happened to him or her that day. That person may have just experienced a rude salesperson that wouldn't stop hassling him or her or received a parking ticket and now looking for the next excuse to release his or her frustrations—you just never know. So never take people's responses personally. The other way to view rejection is to see it as a good thing. This game is a sorting process; *we aren't here to convince people but rather to find people who want time and financial freedom or to improve their lives with our products.* Here is a new perspective: do you think a shop owner takes it to heart and is offended every time someone walks in and doesn't buy anything? Absolutely not. That's because he or she knows and understands the laws of sales.

We must also view all supposed failures and rejections as lessons. Yes, the reality is that we can't sign up everyone, no matter who we are. We should adopt that mind-set, but at the same time ask ourselves what we could have done better. What was good? What needs improvement? But at the end of the day, every experience adds to your experiences, and that is priceless.

15. Building Leaders, Not Followers

"The job of a leader is to grow more leaders." —Robin Sharma

In network marketing, if you fail to build and duplicate leaders, you wind up owning a stressful job! The goal of the business is not to be working sixty hours per week ten years in. Rather, the idea is to create "beach money." With beach money, you can live anywhere in the world with a phone and laptop or laptop and do a few events a year: maybe a couple of training webinars and some coaching in your own time.

Often people come into this business and get it all wrong. They like the idea of being the boss and the center of attention, and they love people needing them to do everything (they mistake this for love). They want to be "*the man*," and they forget about empowering and duplicating leaders.

Here is the other thing I have found: if you're not duplicating your reps, they will usually lose interest. Not many people just want to be the employee. They want to be empowered; they want to have tasks, to present, to speak, and to receive recognition. So if you are the leader and you're hogging the limelight, people will soon resent you and eventually fall off.

Now in saying that, of course not everyone wants to be a leader of a big team and speak at company conventions, and you need these people too. You need a large group of people who are happy being part of the team and collecting their five-hundred-dollar monthly check. They love being part of a community of people who are striving to improve themselves and chasing their dreams. These people are the heart and soul of the industry as well. We need big leaders; we need reps with smaller goals; and of course, we need customers too.

My ultimate goal has always been to set up an organization that allows me to be very lazy in the long term. I had read a lot of business books that all taught me the same thing: you want to end up working on the business, not in it! Now did I walk into this business and put my feet up and micromanage? Of course not! Most people begin to micromanage far too early. *Nothing fails like success!* Success often makes us lazy; it gives us an illusion that we are doing better than we actually are. Often newbies get a couple of reps on board, achieve a tiny bit of success, and think that their job is done, and that they can sit back and play the CEO game. This will come back to bite you on the butt very quickly. Great generals throughout history were the ones in the trenches, leading from the front. So did I do ten meetings a day starting out? Yes! Did I miss going to the gym for two weeks straight? Many times. Did I neglect family and friends for periods? Yes and yes. And was it all worth it? Absolutely.

I believe you have to work out of balance for a period of time to live in balance for the rest of your life. Don't become complacent too soon and never stop bringing in new business. Lead from the front. The good news is that when you reach a point in your business where you are driving exotic cars and hanging out at cafes and resorts all day, people will invite *themselves*, and your business will grow with ease. This took a lot longer to happen than I expected. I imagined that when I was making $150,000 a year from home and driving a new Mercedes, the attraction effect would kick in, when in reality it didn't until I was earning double that. But it will happen if you stick it out long enough.

16. Tracking

"Numbers don't lie." —*Anonymous*

Like all business, network marketing is a numbers game, and numbers don't lie. The industry's current top earner, Holton Buggs, is said to be the best numbers analyst and spends hours each week on examining them.

In a traditional business, you look at key performance numbers like this:

Leads x Conversion x Average Order Price x Retention = Revenue

In network marketing terms, this means:

Leads (combined number of invitations per week in your organization) x
Conversion (the strength of the presentation and follow-up) x
Average order price (same) x
Retention (number of auto ships) =
Revenue (our total profits)

If your profit (income) isn't where you want it to be, you can look at these key factors and find out where exactly you are falling short. This is why it is so important that all of your leaders understand the power of numbers. I have all my key leaders submit their team's weekly number of invitations, house presentations being held, one-on-ones completed, and overall volume. This way we can always clearly identify which areas need improvement.

If the conversions are extremely low, you know to look at the presentation layout that the team is using or even how they are following up. If retention is low, you can look at system attendance numbers, etc. If leads are lacking, you know to go back to invitation training and maybe run a competition for the highest number of invitations. The numbers are everything: a ten-person team can out earn a one-hundred-person team if the ten people are sticking to their numbers. For example, if the ten reps all commit to and execute fifty invitations per week, they have a total of five hundred. If the one hundred reps don't thoroughly track their numbers, they will realistically only do three to four invitations per week each, giving them a combined total of only three hundred to four hundred. This happens far too often in network marketing because often only the new people are inviting. If this happens, the total number of invitations in your team never actually grows, and the new rep just replaces the old rep that used to invite. The key to this business is to stick to and execute the numbers because it's like the universe has an invisible bank that adds up your team's work.

If you want to make real business money, then treat it like a real business. Big businesspeople know their numbers inside out, and top network marketing teams do too!

17. The Law of Association

"You are the average of the five people you spend the most time with." —*Jim Rohn*

The law of association suggests that you become the average of the five people closest to you. If you believe in the idea that we are all energy and all connected as one, then this law holds a lot of truth. Your habits are generated by the programming from your environment, and the five closest people to you are a big part of that environment and, therefore, program your subconscious mind without you even knowing it. No matter how strong you are, it will affect you in some way. If you surround a positive person with five negative people for a long enough period of time, he or she might only be affected by a small amount, but a weaker person will be as negative as the other five before you know it.

What if your five are toxic and negative? Now I know many of you are sitting there thinking, "But Dave! I live at home with my negative, loser family. I can't afford to move out, so I am doomed!" Well ultimately we need to create an exit strategy, but in the meantime, we need to brainwash you with good stuff (everyone's brain needs a good washing). Immerse yourself in your favorite audios, have conversations with your favorite authors by reading their books, and make those great people the five you listen to most of all. We are truly blessed today to have such incredible access to the greatest people in history. With the knowledge and wisdom that we now have available at our fingertips, we can excel and advance much more quickly than ever before. But also make a conscious effort to spend time with people who are going places. Ask your successful friends and family to meet up with you for coffee or go to events where people are growing and working on themselves. But best of all, work on becoming better yourself, and you will naturally attract better people into your life.

Despite what I have just said, don't turn your back on your negative friends or family. I'm sure they have done well by you, and they may even love you. But for the sake of your own future, you need to slowly distance yourself and limit the time that you spend with them each week. If you want to fly, you have to let go of the weights that are dragging you down. If some people get upset, remember that you have to crack a few eggs to make an omelette. Success isn't easy, and letting go of toxic relationships can be hard. But remember that life only responds to those who make sacrifices, and a life of mental toxicity is much harder to live with than the difficulty of distancing yourself from old friends.

As I mentioned earlier, your subconscious mind has been programmed by everyone from your parents to your school teachers and society. You can't change this, but the good news is that the most influential programming (that which you can now control) comes from within your inner circle. You can see it take effect in every area of life. Recently I my buddy, a successful body builder, came to live with me. Before long I had broken all of my personal records—coincidence? I think not. I was continually surrounded by someone who was pushing me, setting the standard, and raising the lid on what I thought was possible. So be very careful about who you surround yourself with, and do your best to "brainwash" yourself with the ideologies of the people whose lives you want to be living.

When I was getting started I made a big effort to get around the top earners in the company, build relationships with them, and pick their brains daily! No one asks enough questions these days—other than, "So what's the secret?"—and this is why people take so long to grow their organization. I remember following the founder around on my first company retreat like a lost puppy dog. But I wasn't just aimlessly following or, like we would say at school, being the "teacher's pet." I was taking notes and asking questions about scenarios because I wanted to enter the mind of someone who was already at such a high level of success. Oddly enough, a couple of years later he became one of the top five people that I spoke to most regularly, and I benefited greatly from that close relationship. It was if I was having my body charged with energy on a daily basis.

18. Killing the Selling Stigma

"Everyone lives by selling something." —Robert Louis Stevenson

One objection you will face quite regularly is: "I don't want to sell." In fact people will be world class at selling you the idea that they can't sell. And some may be so good at selling you on this idea that you will actually believe them! People attach the idea of selling to the notion that they are forcing someone to buy something that he or she doesn't want. But we are not in that game! Fortunately in this business, if it's done correctly, we aren't in the selling game at all. Time and time again I have seen top salespeople come into this industry and do quite poorly. Randy Gage says it, and I've certainly experienced it myself. Hard-selling, hard-closing, NLP, hypnosis, all that fancy stuff—none of it works here. And even if it did, it wouldn't duplicate. I'm not sure if anyone understands the science behind it, but there's a bad energy within the group when someone is hard-sold. It's as if the new rep has buyer's remorse and never recovers enough to grow the business. Whatever the reason, know that being a classic salesperson does not work.

Our goal is not to sell to anyone; we are in the game of sorting and educating. We are looking for people who want what we have, and then it's our role to provide them with enough education on the topic for them to make a decision for themselves. So the next time someone says, "I can't sell," say, "Great! If you could, we would have to spend the next two months unlearning those skills."

While that is the easy response, I don't have a problem with selling (educating). Every leap forward by mankind—every concept, every revelation and invention, every piece of artwork, and every life-changing movie—has been sold heavily to us. But because we see its value, we automatically dismiss the fact that it is selling. So if you believe in the opportunity that you are offering and in what you are doing, you will quickly erase any bad feelings toward the scary S word: *selling* is good!

19. Dealing with Problems

"Every negative is a positive. The bad things that happen to me, I somehow make them good. That means you can't do anything to hurt me."
—50 Cent

As an entrepreneur or business person, you are in the business of solving a global problem. In network marketing this is even more apparent as you deal with a wide range of people's problems. But fortunately, it's not forever. It's only until you have built a great enough depth of leaders to screen the majority of problems.

"He who handles the most problems wins" is the memorable quote that my up-line shared with me in my early days. Fortunately it stuck in my

head and probably saved me from throwing in the towel. I was involved in opening a new company in a new country, and those who have had a similar experience will understand how difficult it can be and how many problems you are faced with. For us it paid off, but for many it doesn't. This quotation turned out to be extremely important because it got me through all of the drama, problems, and disappointments along the way. Every time the going got tough, I replayed that quotation in my head. I said to myself, "This is all just a test, and if you can get through it, you will have everything." That's the power of self-talk. Little conversations in your head like that can play a huge role in your success.

Everyone has their favorite uncle or ultratalented friend who lives in another country and is going to be the next big star. Unfortunately your up-line has already heard this story five hundred times, and every time it is too hard, and the particular person doesn't come through with the goods. Can it be done? Absolutely. Is it worth the time and stress? Yes it is! But would I recommend it? It really depends on how committed the particular rep is. He or she needs to be ready to potentially commit years of work to opening up a new country. This will all depend on the logistics of registering the product and the company in that country. For some companies this will be extremely simple, and for others it will be a long, grueling, and extremely expensive process. Every country has different laws, and in some countries your product might simply not be a possibility. Another question to consider is, why go through all of that stress when you can build it where you are?

In the business of network marketing, as your team grows, you will come into contact with thousands of people. That means thousands of problems, dramas, stories, hypochondriacs—the works. You will see the good side of humanity, and you will see the bad side. But remember, in any situation in any business, an entrepreneur's role is to handle problems by finding solutions. So give your up-line a helping hand and don't go to him or her with your long list of problems. Take charge yourself and try to find a solution. The goal of life isn't to try to eliminate problems (the only people with no problems are dead). The goal is to grow bigger than any problem. You want to grow so big that what would have once derailed you now becomes a minor irritation.

20. Secrets of Success

"There is no elevator to success; you have to take the stairs." —Unknown

The truth about achieving the highest level of success in life and business is the truth that none of us want to hear. It certainly wasn't what got you along to see your first opportunity presentation. Unfortunately there is no secret, and there are no shortcuts. The universe responds to what is deserved, not what is needed or wanted. The only secret you will come across is the need to work your ass off at a high intensity for a lengthy period of time. I use the word *intensity* because just showing up isn't enough—you need to turn up! Turn up with passion, enthusiasm, excitement—that's the showing up, that counts. Just attending doesn't count. The other secret to success isn't as sexy as what we would hope for either: master the basics! Throughout my career I have steered away from the basics and attempted to reinvent the wheel many times. We all think, "It can't be that easy," but the elite performers of all industries have spent focused time on mastering the simple basics.

So essentially, hard work is "the catch" of this entire industry. You can live every dream and achieve every goal you ever imagined, but the road up the mountain is tough, and you can't be dropped off by a helicopter! Is it hard? Absolutely it is, but once you realize that life is hard you can choose which type of hard you want to work with. Let's look at what is easy: being broke is easy; being a fat slob is easy; being negative and complaining all day is easy; sitting back and having a go at the ones doing it is easy; and staying the same is easy. All of these things are easy in the short-term but extremely hard in the long-term. *So embrace the "hard now" because it leads to the "easy later."* It's a simple choice.

The million-dollar earners in this industry have mastered the profession, and to fill you in on a little secret, the story that they worked ten hours a week and just followed the system to become wealthy is trash! They completely committed themselves and became immersed in their work. They may have had a difficult few years, maybe even a difficult ten, but the ones that reach mastery level in this industry live like kings.

"I believe in total immersion, if you want to be rich, you have to program your mind to be rich. You have to unlearn all the thoughts that were making you poor and replace them with new thoughts—rich thoughts" (Jordan Belfort, the "Wolf of Wall Street"). If you look at anyone in life who has truly amazing results to show for himself or herself, you will discover that there was a time when he or she hyperfocused and became obsessed to become a master at what he or she did. But these levels of results aren't for everyone; wealth isn't for everyone; success isn't for everyone; it might not be for you.

21. The Importance of Fun

"You can be childlike without being childish. A child always wants to have fun. Ask yourself, 'Am I having fun?'" —Christopher Meloni

Children are unprogrammed human beings in their purest form, and I believe that we have much to learn from them. They are playful and full of laughter; they dance and sing when everyone is watching; and they have an abundance of love and affection. I read this week that the average child laughs four hundred times a day, and the average adult only laughs fifteen times. I think it's fair to say that we're doing this thing called "living" drastically wrong, guys.

Now I know it's very easy for me to say, "Just relax and have fun, guys!" And I must admit that when I started I was ruthless and had zero fun whatsoever. But it's so important to lighten up and have fun during your presentations because people will be far more attracted to your business. Enjoying the journey and laughing when you get a stupid objection or aggression from a naysayer will make the whole experience far more worthwhile because, at the end of the day, we are all going to leave this planet with nothing anyway. When dealing with any problem I always ask myself, "On the last day of my life, will this matter?"

Steve Jobs encapsulated this brilliantly in a speech about success and his journey with Apple. He said, "It's really hard. And you have to do it over a sustained period of time. So if you don't love it, if you're not having fun doing it, you don't really love it, you're going to give up." I think that this rings very true in network marketing as well. People can often put so much pressure on themselves and get so angry and frustrated that it all becomes too much, and they break down and quit. I was far too serious when I started out. My mentality was, "Why would you be smiling and having fun if you were broke?" Maybe that mentality served me; maybe it didn't, but today I am much more relaxed. I still get frustrated and disappointed when targets are missed, and it tends to set off a firecracker, and I work twice as hard. But the difference these days is that I detach myself emotionally and go to bed at night knowing that it's all part of a process, and I rest at ease. I think that I'm a much better person to be around today because I've developed a healthy balance between being ultraserious and having fun. There needs to be a balance, and it's possible that we burned way too many reps early on by not making the business fun.

Social activities are a vital part of network marketing, and if it's all business and money, money, money, you quickly lose the human element. And money won't build bonds and relationships deep enough to reach the highest level of success. So smile more, laugh more, do things that make you happy in your down time, and remember that smiling and having fun are the most attractive qualities you can project in an attraction marketing game.

"What's the point of reaching the top of the mountain if you don't enjoy yourself along the way?"

22. Putting It All together

"You will never change your life until you change something you do daily. The secret of your success is found in your daily routine." —Darren Hardy

We often read an inspirational book, or we go to a motivational seminar, and we are ready to change the world. But by the time Monday afternoon arrives, we are in the same state of mind as we started. We are still stuck with our old habits, and as a result, we don't change. Despite there being hundreds of solutions available to us in the self-development world, only the rare few ever reach the highest levels of success.

The only way that we can have any hope of making some serious long-term changes is if we practice this stuff daily, for a long enough period of time for a habit to be developed (which is around sixty days, not twenty-one, like many people think).

So here is the daily ritual that I still use today. I came up with this after reading hundreds of books and having completed many self-development programs. It's a compilation that I feel is well rounded, fast, and effective.

The ritual takes approximately forty-five minutes, so you may need to set your alarm clock a little earlier than usual. (This will get easier and become a habit also.)

Waking up:
Breathing: Spend your first few minutes breathing in long, deep breaths. No one breathes like we are supposed to, and doing it properly can help to oxygenate the cells and balance the body. I like the technique that goes like this: four seconds in through the mouth, four-second hold, four-second exhale through the mouth. Do at least ten sets of these to start the day.

Nutrition:
Liquid nutrition is a crucial part of getting off to a good start. The body will absorb nutritious drinks most effectively early on an empty stomach, so make the most of this. I like super greens-style shakes, teas, or freshly squeezed juices. You are what you eat, so start ingesting goodness early, and it will positively affect your entire day.

Reprogram—read/watch/listen:
As we discussed earlier, we need to change the subconscious programming that we've received throughout our lives. So do it with your favorite book, motivational video, or audio recording. I estimate that fifteen minutes a day is all you need. (I do more throughout the day.)

Gratitude:
List ten things in your life for which you are grateful. If you are really committed, write them down on paper because it's said to have a more powerful universal effect. If not, just visualize.

Visualize the short-term:
Spend approximately five minutes visualizing the end of a great day. Write down five things that you have accomplished.

Visualise a year ahead:
Spend five minutes visualizing your life twelve months from now. Be specific about what you will become, what you will accomplish, and what impact you will make. Focus on health, wealth, self, and relationships.

Affirmations:
Spend a couple of minutes writing out approximately ten of your favorite mantras. I like to start them all with the powerful words: *I am.* (If you are stuck, go back to the successful people characteristics exercise and copy the traits of the people you admire.)

Daily actions, top ten:
Commit to daily goal setting. Write down ten outcome-based goals that you wish to accomplish. For network marketers, here are your first five:

I will invite __ people today.
I will make __ presentations today.
I will make __ follow-ups today.
I will make __ calls to my team today.
I will meet __ new people today and get their names.

Play some inspirational music or audio as you begin getting dressed and getting ready for your day.

Download my free worksheet at davenelson.tv/freestuff.

Final Message

"There is no greater thing you can do with your life and your work than follow your passions—in a way that serves the world and you."

—SIR RICHARD BRANSON

EVERY OPPORTUNITY AND TOOL THAT YOU NEED to live out your dreams is at your fingertips; the rest is truly up to you and only you. So I want to finish with a story that I believe is a great example of most people's lives and the reason why most people never reach greatness:

A man walks to work each day, and each day he walks past the same house and sees the same thing: a dog sitting on the porch, crying. Day after day, week after week, the same dog continues to sit in the same spot and cry the same whimpers.

Then one day, on his way to work the man sees what appears to be the dog's owner. He stops and calls out to the owner, "Good morning, may I ask what is wrong with the poor dog? He has been on the porch for months, crying day in, day out. Is he okay?" The owner replies, "Yes, he is in pain. He impaled himself on a nail, and it is becoming infected."

The man then says to the owner, "Then why doesn't he get up off the nail?" And the owner replies, "Because it is hurting enough for him to complain about it but not enough for him to get up and do something about it."

And that, ladies and gentleman, is the sad story of most people's lives. We live in quiet desperation and do so because we have conditioned ourselves to endure the pain. We have accepted the fact that "this is life," and we take the path most walked, which appears to be the easiest option, but it usually ends in tears.

So I urge you to get off the nail! Get off the nail before it becomes infected. The longer you leave it, the more the infection will spread, until it's too late.

You may not be ready; I understand that, but the fact is that you never will be. Storms aren't going to pass, and mountains aren't going to move for your perfect opportunity to get started. You need to take action now. Network marketing has a great system; your company has a great product; but the rest is up to you.

So get off the nail, set your goals, take risks, fail miserably, and then get back up and go again. Get laughed at, keep pushing the envelope, and go live out the endless possibilities that your life is meant to hold!

In times of depression or great struggle, the world turns, and the universe rewards the brave ones—the ones willing to take off the blinkers and step outside of the norm. The education system, the work force, and society often create followers—people not really doing what they love and just being herded through life, doing what they are told to do and thinking what they are told to think. But the universe doesn't reward these people. It rewards the rebels, the visionaries, and the crusaders.

Crusades start from the streets and in the suburbs—with the people who unite together for a better way and for a deeper cause. They gain momentum and put a dent in the universe. Right now, we have a better way. We have solutions that the world desperately needs.

The world needs more dreamers, more risk takers, and more visionaries— the world needs you!

Your partner in prosperity,

Dave Nelson

Made in the USA
Middletown, DE
21 August 2016